2101412
EDSEC
8.49

FICIAL TE

THIS IS HISTORY!

Lost in Time

A KEY STAGE 3 DEVELOPMENT STUDY

IAN DAWSON

JOHN MURRAY

The Schools History Project

The Project was set up in 1972, with the aim of improving the study of History for students aged 13–16. This involved a reconsideration of the ways in which History contributes to the educational needs of young people. The Project devised new objectives, new criteria for planning and developing courses, and the materials to support them. New examinations, requiring new methods of assessment, also had to be developed. These have continued to be popular. The advent of GCSE in 1987 led to the expansion of Project approaches into other syllabuses.

The Schools History Project has been based at Trinity and All Saints College, Leeds, since 1978, from where it supports teachers through a biennial Bulletin, regular INSET, an annual Conference and a website (www.tasc.ac.uk/shp).

Since the National Curriculum was drawn up in 1991, the Project has continued to expand its publications, bringing its ideas to courses for Key Stage 3 as well as a range of GCSE and A level specifications.

Note: The wording and sentence structure of some written sources have been adapted and simplified to make them accessible to all pupils, while faithfully preserving the sense of the original.

Words printed in SMALL CAPITALS are defined in the Glossary on page 114.

Edge Hill College Library ERL
Author Dawson, I
Class No. 941
Book No. 618885

© Ian Dawson 2001

First published in 2001
by John Murray (Publishers) Ltd
50 Albemarle Street
London W1S 4BD

All rights reserved. No part of this publication may be reproduced in any material form (including photocopying or storing in any medium by electronic means and whether or not transiently or incidentally to some other use of this publication) without the written permission of the publisher, except in accordance with the provisions of the Copyright, Designs and Patents Act 1988 or under the terms of a licence issued by the Copyright Licensing Agency.

Layouts by Amanda Hawkes
Artwork by Art Construction, Richard Duszczak, Tony Randell, Edward Ripley, Martin Salisbury
Typeset in Goudy by Wearset, Boldon, Tyne and Wear
Printed and bound in Great Britain by Butler and Tanner, Frome and London

A catalogue entry for this book is available from the British Library

ISBN 0 7195 8557 0
Teachers' Resource Book ISBN 0 7195 8558 9

◆ Contents

SECTION 1

WHEN WOULD YOU MOST LIKE TO LIVE?

One thousand years of British social history

1.1 LOST IN TIME

As your time capsule lurches out of control, think about when in the past you'd most like to live, and why

Today's fast-breaking news is that a time capsule containing a class of schoolchildren is missing, lost in time. The capsule is from Newtown High School. On board are nearly thirty children, all aged about eleven, and their history teacher, Mr Mullins.

They were returning from a school trip to Ancient Rome when there was a computer failure. They cannot speak to their school but, more importantly, they do not seem to be able to return to the 21st century.

Worried parents say that they warned the school about taking such a long journey in an old time capsule. The school is due to buy a new capsule next month, after a year-long fund-raising drive by the Parent–Teacher Association.

We will update you on this story as soon as we have more news.

25 Oct. 2015
TV NEWS
We can't get home to 2015.
I wish we hadn't left Mr Mullins behind in Rome.
Can't we go back and get him?
No point, that lion will have eaten him by now.
Danger! Danger! Danger! Computer failure. My database is leaking vital information. I cannot recognise any date beginning with 2. We cannot re-enter the 21st century.

Activity

Your adventure in time is about to begin. Your time capsule will land sometime in the past. If you cannot fix your computer problem and collect more fuel, then you will have to stay there – for ever.

a) Discuss how you will decide whether you would like to live in the past. Think about what you will need and what will make your life happy there.

b) Make a list of the things that will help you to decide.

◆ Choosing your future – in the past!

Did you make a list of criteria to decide whether you would be happy living in the past? Criteria – perhaps you don't know that word, although you use criteria all the time. For example, you use criteria if you are choosing where to go on holiday. You think about whether you would make friends there, whether there is a beach, whether there are good theme parks, whether the weather is good. Those are all criteria – reasons for choosing or deciding something.

On the opposite page you can see criteria for deciding whether you would be happy to live in the past if you couldn't get home. The criteria are divided into groups which make up a **sorting grid**. Each time you land in the past you will fill in a sorting grid like the one shown. You will put in information about living at that time and this will help you to decide whether you want to live in that period of history. Each criterion has an icon. On each page we will show icons to guide you in collecting your data.

ACTIVITY

1. Look at the five criteria on page 5. Which of these criteria do you think will be most important in making your decision?
2. You will use the pendulum below to record your feelings about living in the past. When your visit to a period of history ends, and you have completed your sorting grid, you will mark on your copy of this pendulum what you feel about living in that period of history.

I would prefer to live here rather than in the 21st century.
I do not really want to live here but I could put up with it if I had to.
I would hate to live here.

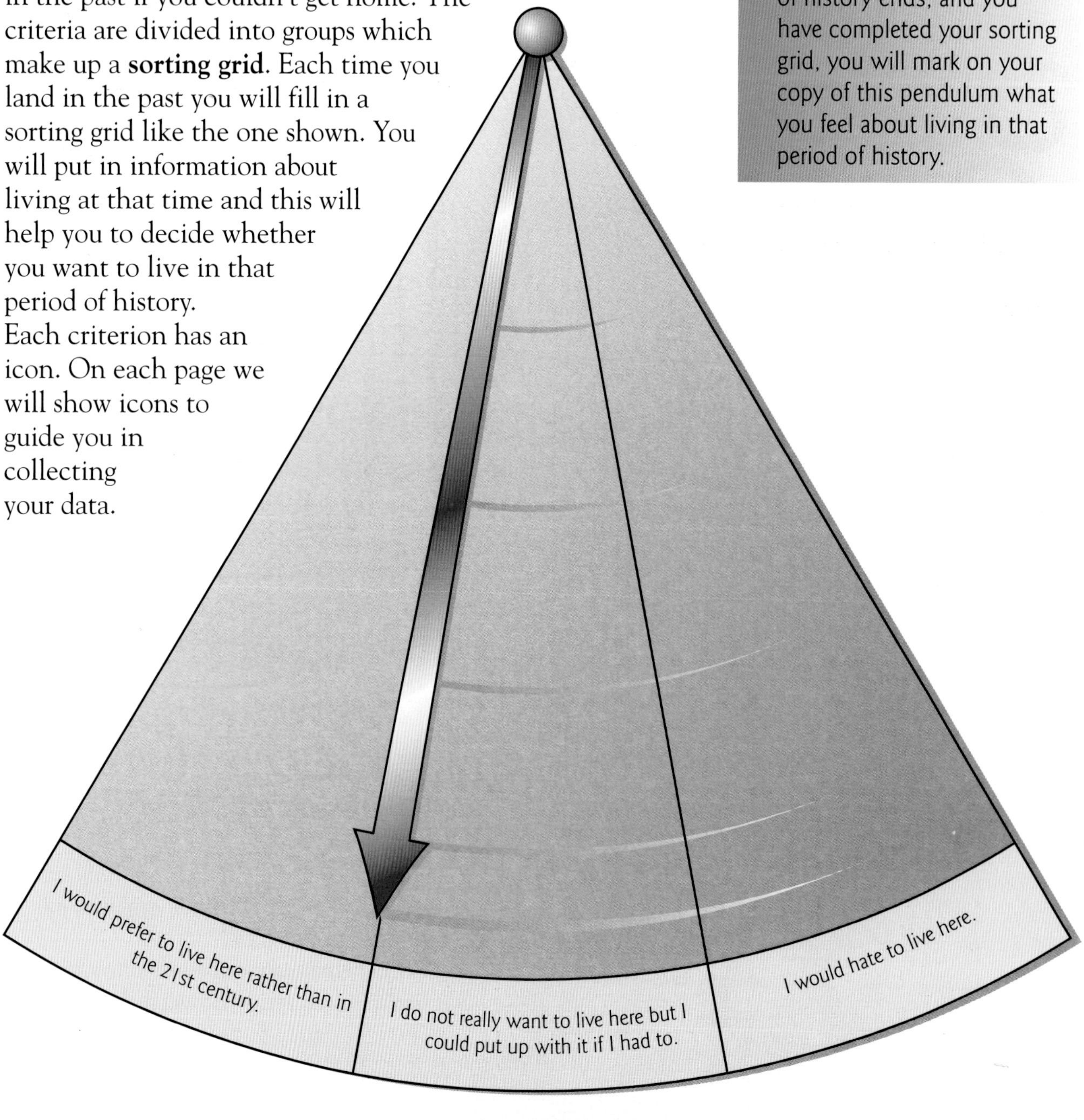

SORTING GRID

Criterion 1 How comfortable will I be?

Icon:

Comfort

Food

Drink

Clothing

Light and heat

Housing and furniture

Clean water; toilets

Energy and fuel

Transport

Criterion 2 How much work will I have to do?

Icon:

Work

All day

Part-time

Just at school

Slavery

Rates of pay

Help from machinery

Criterion 3 What can I do for enjoyment?

Icon:

Enjoyment

Games

Sports

Music

Books

Holidays

Visits

Criterion 4 What dangers and suffering will there be?

Icon:

Danger

Crimes

Help from police

Medicines and hospitals

Diseases

Life-expectancy

Criterion 5 How free and equal will I be?

Icon:

Freedom

Are women and men equal?

Can I vote in elections?

Are minorities persecuted?

Are all religions tolerated?

Can you marry whoever you want?

It's time to land. What date will it be? You'll find out on the next page . . .

1.2 LIFE WITH THE LUTTRELLS

◆ Meet Sir Geoffrey

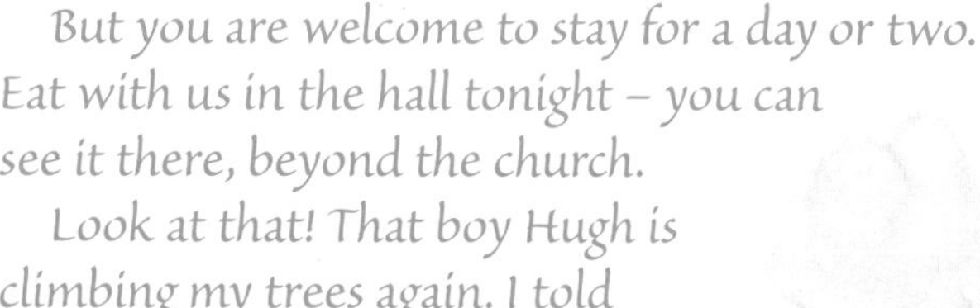

Welcome to Gerneham. You can stay here for a few days – but no longer. There are too many people already and not enough food.

There were only half as many people living here when King John gave this village to my family. They could feed everyone from the crops grown in one field. If they used the Mill Field, they left South Field FALLOW. *Turn and turn about each year. Rest the soil and you get better crops next time, everyone knows that.*

Now we need every strip of land to grow food. The new farming ideas from Walter of Henley's book help us but everything depends on the weather. With the right mix of sun and rain we get a good harvest, but if the weather's poor the villagers go very hungry. Pray God we'll never have another harvest as bad as the one fifteen years ago. It rained all year, drowning the crops. There was nothing to harvest. People starved to death all over the country.

But you are welcome to stay for a day or two. Eat with us in the hall tonight – you can see it there, beyond the church.

Look at that! That boy Hugh is climbing my trees again. I told him, if I catch him he'll be in the stocks. Over the page I'll show you how I deal with troublemakers.

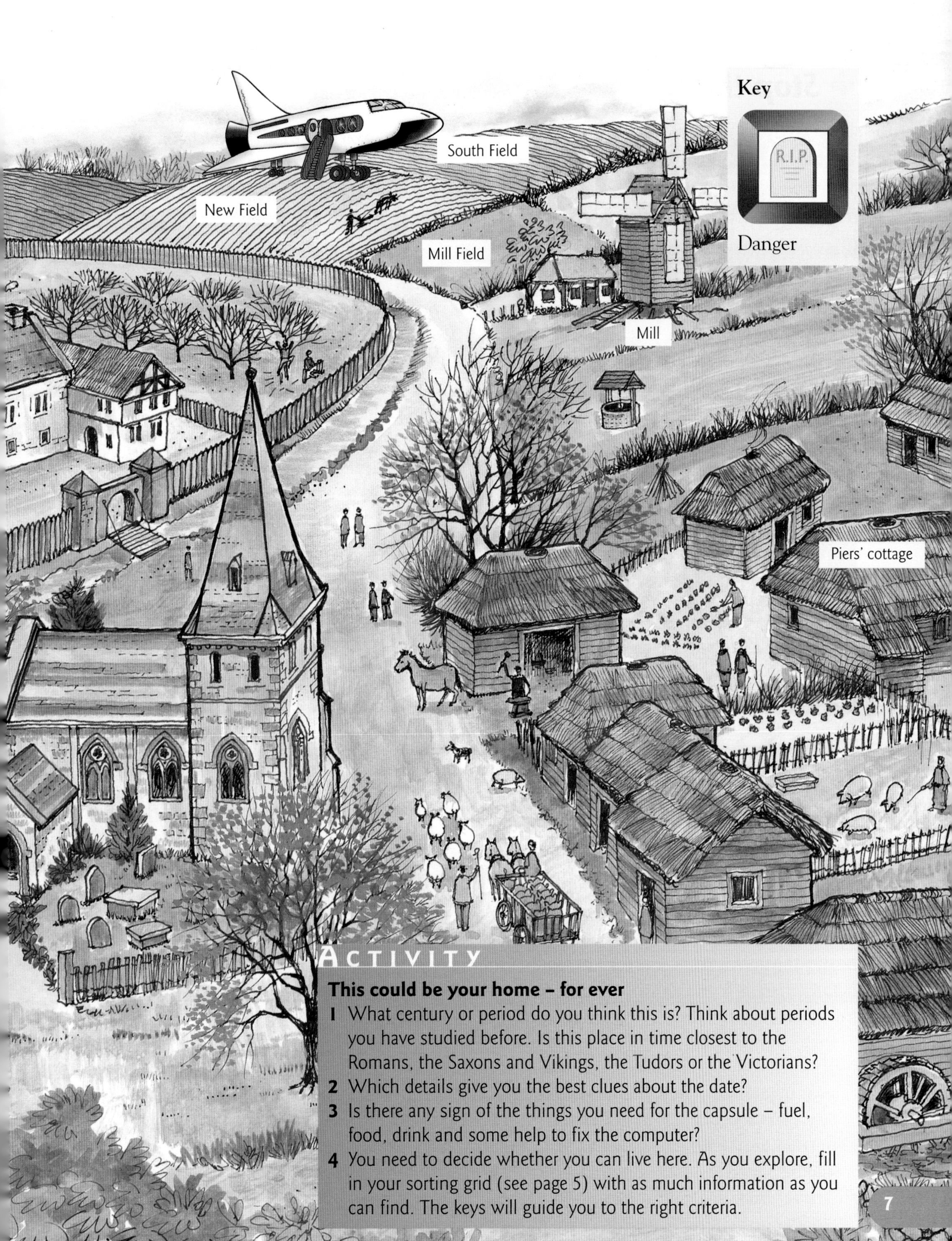

ACTIVITY

This could be your home – for ever

1. What century or period do you think this is? Think about periods you have studied before. Is this place in time closest to the Romans, the Saxons and Vikings, the Tudors or the Victorians?
2. Which details give you the best clues about the date?
3. Is there any sign of the things you need for the capsule – fuel, food, drink and some help to fix the computer?
4. You need to decide whether you can live here. As you explore, fill in your sorting grid (see page 5) with as much information as you can find. The keys will guide you to the right criteria.

Stop thief!

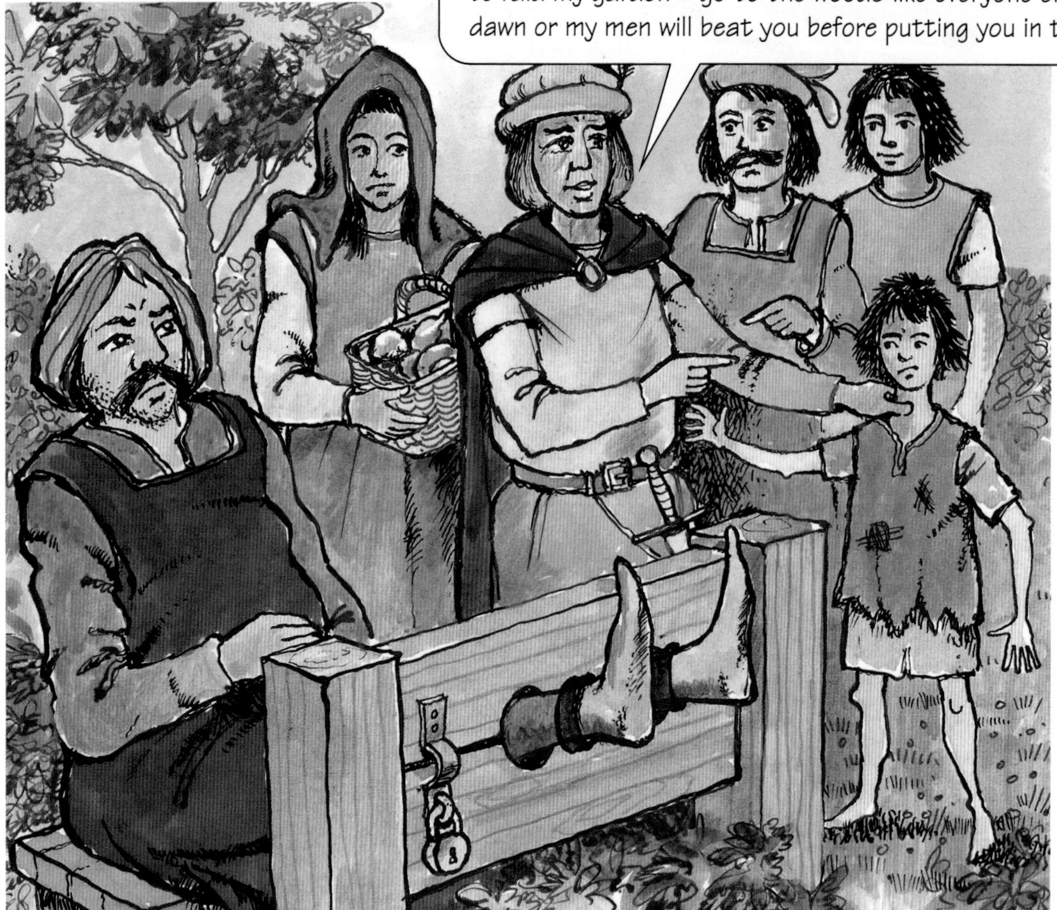

Tomorrow, Hugh, you'll spend all day in these stocks. That's what I promised if I caught you stealing from my garden again. In the summer it's cherries and apples, now it's firewood. You don't need to raid my garden – go to the woods like everyone else. Be here at dawn or my men will beat you before putting you in the stocks.

Sir Geoffrey

The man in the stocks is William. He's there because he let his cow stray and break down a hedge and he can't pay his three pence fine. But I've let his wife bring him food – after all, if he is ill he won't be able to plough my land next week. Most cases in the village court are about simple everyday problems like that – villagers letting animals trample other people's crops or girls getting married without my permission.

Thefts happen mostly at harvest time when houses are empty because everyone is working in the fields. If the thief is one of the villagers and he's never stolen before, then he'll probably just be fined, but we have to be harsh with PERSISTENT *thieves. Last year, Father Thomas saw a stranger climbing out of his window. Thomas shouted 'Stop thief' to begin the* HUE AND CRY *and the villagers caught him. He'd stolen Thomas's best leather shoes. It turned out that he was one of a gang of thieves. The sheriff's men took him to the King's judges in Lincoln. He was hanged.*

Five years ago, in 1325, a villager was murdered. Too much ale led to a brawl. John tried to stab Roger. Roger fought back and killed John. We were afraid Roger would be hanged but the King's judges freed him because he was defending himself. He's never been in a fight since!

Now, enough of these stories. Come indoors and meet my wife, Lady Agnes.

◆ *In the bed chamber*

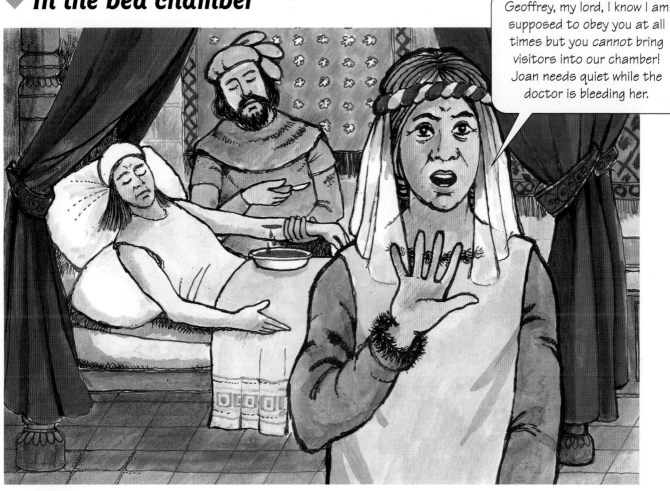

Geoffrey, my lord, I know I am supposed to obey you at all times but you *cannot* bring visitors into our chamber! Joan needs quiet while the doctor is bleeding her.

Lady Agnes

Oh, I'm sorry. That must sound rude to you but Joan has been my maid for many years and I am worried about her. She's been ill for a few days now so we sent to Lincoln for a doctor. He has checked the colour of her urine against his chart and he says her HUMOURS are out of balance. She needs BLEEDING today, while the moon is in the right quarter of the sky.

Normally I treat all the illnesses among the servants. Of course, I don't pull teeth – that's the blacksmith's job – but I'll mix a potion of feverfew for headaches, marjoram for bruises or honey for sores. I learn a lot from old Alice in the village. She knows just which herbs to use for every illness and, of course, the villagers always call her when a baby is born.

Oh dear, I'm chattering on. Geoffrey says I talk too much. Go into the hall. Beatrice, our daughter-in-law, will find you food and drink. We arranged for her to marry our son, Andrew, when they were quite small. She's sixteen now. We may have our first grandchild soon, if God is kind. I do pray for a healthy baby. So many little ones die young. I've had six children and I've been blessed that four have lived.

Oh, what am I thinking of, gossiping on when poor Joan is ill. Go and find Beatrice (on the next page). She'll look after you.

Dinner!

Third course – swan, pigeon pie, cod and oysters

Yes, I'm Beatrice. Did Lady Agnes keep you talking? She chatters on but she's kind. So is Sir Geoffrey, although he tries to sound gruff. He's godfather to five of the servants' children. Not many lords would agree to that.

Lady Agnes has never beaten us, even when Andrew, my husband, couldn't remember all the lessons about eating politely. Lady Agnes told us time and again how to behave at table – 'don't blow your nose with your fingers; don't scratch; don't blow on your food; wash your hands before eating; always have clean nails'. In the end she had William, the steward, write out all the lessons so we could read them ourselves. Watch Andrew at dinner – his manners are perfect now. Just what he'll need when he goes to the King's court.

Dinner will be at midday. John, the cook, says there will be three courses and you'll get a loaf of white bread, not like that gritty brown bread most of the villagers eat. Sir Geoffrey likes visitors to admire his new PEWTER plates. *You* won't be using them though – a dried bread TRENCHER is good enough for you, but you might get some hot spiced wine: it's a lot better than ale in this weather.

John's also made puddings and a marzipan subtlety for the end of the meal – I do love marzipan. Last time he made one that looked just like the castle at Lincoln. I don't know what this one's like – he's making it in the kitchen and that's in a different building because of the danger of fire.

Second course – rabbit, beef and salted herrings

First course – chicken, pheasant and eels

Now I must go to bathe and dress. My maid, Alice, will have the tub full of hot water for me. I've got two gowns trimmed with squirrel fur, and Andrew has promised me a new scarlet gown from Lincoln fair. You wouldn't believe how many gowns Lady Agnes has – nearly twenty! She has new clothes made in the latest fashions at least four times a year. She has to look her best at Christmas and Whit and the other feast days. Even young Isabel gets new clothes twice a year. She's Andrew's younger sister. Eight years old she is now, such a pretty thing, always smiling. Sir Geoffrey has promised her to the convent when she is a little older. Imagine, Isabel a nun.

Are you staying the night? Sir Geoffrey and my lady have their own chamber and so do Andrew and I. There's a guest chamber for important visitors but I expect you'll sleep here in the hall with the servants. Ask William, the steward, for a straw pallet and he'll show you where to sleep. If you need the GARDEROBE*, it's over the main chamber.*

Be careful with the candles and don't waste them either. We use six pounds of candles a day in winter. I'm glad I don't have to make them – the smell of all that pig fat!

I must go.

Do you want to see round the village before dinner? I'll get that boy to show you.

Hugh! Hugh!

Key

Comfort

Freedom

At the fair

Hugh
Key
Enjoyment
No, Sir Geoffrey banned it after young John was killed – tripped over the ball and fell on his own knife. Very messy. Besides the King says we have to practise archery. We're never going to go to France and play football, are we?
No football this year?
Ten eggs for a penny!
A day in the stocks will stop you selling mouldy bread.
New pots and pans sold here!

I hope you'll still be here for the midsummer fair. It lasts four whole days. We have markets every week but the fair is the best. It's the most exciting thing I've ever seen!

Now, Tom, you know gambling is against Church law. Perhaps you'd better give your winnings to the church fund.
Get your new knives here!
Spices, spices from the HOLY LAND – pepper, ginger, saffron…
SPICES
Roast pig – only eightpence
Three roast thrushes – only tuppence!
Silk ribbons – blue, red, choose your colour!
This is the tale of Robin Hood and the monk. Once upon a time . . .

◆ *It's all right for some!*

Piers

God's bones, I hate this! I'm breaking clods of earth for Sir Geoffrey. It breaks my back. I have to do this for Sir Geoffrey just because I'm Piers the VILLEIN. *Two days a week I slave on his land before I get the chance to work my own strips of land. Sir Geoffrey has his horse, his hawks and his armour and it's my work that pays for all his finery.*

My best cow, that's what I had to give him when I took over my father's land. I need his permission for our daughter to marry. I need his permission to leave the village for a day. By St James, at Easter we even give him six eggs, a goose and a chicken, as if he was poor and we had food to spare.

He wouldn't eat the food we have to make do with. Pottage, pottage, pottage, that's all I see. It's a kind of soup made from vegetables from our garden – onions, beans, peas and garlic. Vegetables! If I was rich I'd feast on meat at every meal; there'd be no more vegetables for me. God's bones, I'm lucky to get scraps of bacon or a bit of rabbit poached from Sir Geoffrey's rabbit warren.

You can tell who's a villein and who's free in this village. We villeins wear white cloth. We can't afford cloth dyed some fancy colour. A freeman like Richard there, ploughing the field – he's not tied to Sir Geoffrey. If he wants to go somewhere else he can. No begging permission for him. And he can afford to wear dark clothes

What do I get in return for all my work? A few meals at harvest and on holy days. Not much for being in the fields all hours in all weathers. Just because he *was born a gentleman and* I *was born a villein! Look at the pictures on the church wall. Were there any gentlemen when Adam was in the Garden of Eden or was everybody equal then?*

Moan, moan, moan, that's all that man does! Piers is a good husband but he never stops complaining. I keep telling him that a villein's life isn't as bad as he makes out. At least we do have land, and apples and pears in our garden, eggs from the geese and hens, and honey from our bees. If the harvest is poor, Sir Geoffrey makes sure we have something to eat. Not like those poor cottagers on the edge of the village. They can't grow enough food on their little patches of land so they depend on getting work and earning a few pennies, but these days there's not enough work to go round. They'll starve if there's a poor harvest.

My name is Heloise, by the way. Can you look after the baby while I sweep the floor? There's nowhere to leave her safely. You hear terrible stories of little ones killed crawling into fires or down wells because everyone is too busy to look after them. Our older children have gone to help bring the sheep in from the fields. After that they'll need to collect wood for the fire, enough to last a week. It's a help having children to do chores. I've had seven babies but four died when they were very young.

Now what next? I need to see to the ale: I make a few pennies from brewing it. Later I'll mend some clothes but I hate doing that on dark nights. I can't see the cloth properly, however close I sit to the firelight, and the smoke gets in my eyes. And then there's our meal to get ready. I haven't got time to stand around complaining, not like some!

I've just fetched this water. At least the well isn't frozen – that's when fetching the water gets really hard. Collecting wood and water takes up so much time. If you're going up to the mill (on the next page) could you take this sack of corn for me? Tell the miller it's from Heloise. Now I must get on.

Key

Comfort

Work

Freedom

◆ In the money!

Welcome to the most important building in the village! Everyone needs the mill. Of course, it's not my mill. Sir Geoffrey owns it, and I pay him rent, but I make a tidy sum of money out of the mill. The villagers bring me their sacks of corn and I grind the corn into flour for them. Every bag of flour milled is another coin in my purse. Then the villagers carry their flour away to bake into bread in Sir Geoffrey's ovens.

I've spent a lot of the money I've earned on my house. I had it rebuilt three years ago. I hired the best carpenters in Lincoln, and a slater to give me a good solid roof. It's right next to the mill. Look – the house has a stone base, iron window latches and a good solid door, with iron hinges and the strongest lock and key I could find. Very important that key is, given how much money I collect. Guess how many trees had to be cut down to make this house – thirty! This house will still be here long after I'm gone, not like that house of Piers the villein you were looking at on the last page. That'll only last thirty years, and that's if he's lucky.

The question is – what else am I going to do with my money? I've got no family. My wife died years ago giving birth to our baby. He didn't live either, poor mite. If I keep the money then the new King will want it in taxes. We've only been taxed twice in the last ten years but they say the new King wants WAR WITH FRANCE. He'll collect taxes to pay for the war so I think I'll spend my money before the King wants it!

Do you want to know a secret? Next week I'm going to Lincoln to buy a new horse and then, well, I'm off on a PILGRIMAGE. Why not? I'm a free man. Not like Piers and the other villeins, who can't leave the village even for a day without Sir Geoffrey's permission. I've never been very religious but Father Thomas says it's never too late to make sure of your place in Heaven.

I've already hired a man to run the mill for me while I'm away. First I'll take a look at London and then I'll go to the great cathedral at Canterbury to pray at the tomb of ST THOMAS.

After that, well, I fancy going to take a look at the sea. Sir Geoffrey told me about the sea. Waves of water, he said, rolling in all the time, as far as you can see. Nobody else round here has seen the sea so I reckon it'll be a good story to bring back – *if* I come back that is. Who knows, perhaps I'll get a taste for travel and follow the pilgrim trail to Spain, or even to the holy city of Jerusalem.

Look, here's another customer with a sack of grain. Another sack, another coin in my chest. I must get on. Make sure you call at the church (on the next page). Father Thomas always has a cup of ale for visitors.

◆ Holy days and holidays

Father Thomas

Go on, have some warmed ale to take away the cold. I won't join you. My head still hurts from yesterday's feasting.

Sit and rest yourselves while you drink. I've nothing else to do, so I can stop for a talk. No school today. A few of the freemen send their children to me to learn their letters. They might need them if they want to make their way in the world.

Of course, I didn't teach Sir Geoffrey's children. They went to the grammar school in Lincoln to learn to read and write Latin. They need to be able to read so they can check their accounts and the court records. If they can't read, then how do they know they aren't being cheated by their servants? Mind you, writing isn't so important to the likes of Sir Geoffrey. There's always a servant to do that for him.

I do know a little Latin, enough for the services. The villagers don't understand Latin so I tell them Bible stories in English and they look at the paintings of Heaven and Hell on the wall. It frightens them, that picture of Hell. They always mention it when they confess their sins: they don't want to go to Hell.

I'd rather look at the coloured glass in the windows. You can tell the village has been rich, because these windows must have cost a lot of money. The villagers still pay me their tithes every year, that's a tenth of their crops and animals. I don't keep their tithes myself. It goes to help the poor and elderly and to pay the carpenters to stop the roof leaking. I've got my own land to grow my food.

It's a good life being priest here. I'm always at the centre of whatever is happening. Everyone looks forward to the Church holy days when they don't have to work. There are plenty of them: the festival of our own saint, Saint Andrew, and quite a few others – CANDLEMAS, three days at Easter, Whit, Michaelmas and Christmas, of course.

There's no work over the twelve days of Christmas, then on the first Sunday after Twelfth Night out comes a plough and the boys drag it up here to the church. We bless the plough and pray for a good harvest. To be honest we never stop praying for a good harvest. Then on Plough Monday, the first day of the new working year, the boys drag the plough all round the village. They have great fun cracking whips to get rid of all the evil spirits.

Look, you'd better be getting back to the hall or you won't find a place at the table. Sir Geoffrey always dines well and there's nowhere better than the lord's hall on a cold day. Are those musicians still here?

Come to think of it, I'll go with you. Sir Geoffrey has been telling me of his plans for a new prayer book, a special one to remind him of his family and his servants. I'd like to hear more about it.

Work

Enjoyment

Danger

◆ A visit to town

Sir Geoffrey

I'm in Lincoln, one of the richest towns in the country! There must be six or seven thousand people and it's growing all the time. You could find work here. You might get taken on by one of the merchants from Italy. I know them all. Tell them Sir Geoffrey sent you. They buy and sell anything – wool, cloth, furs, tin. Or you could get work on a ship and sail down river, across to France or the BALTIC.

I'm in Lincoln to borrow money to pay for my new prayer book. It'll cost a lot of money because I want it to be full of pictures as well as prayers. My family used to borrow money from the Jews. Old Aaron was one of the richest men in England – until King Edward threw him and all the other Jews out of the country forty years ago. The King made a fortune by doing that. The Jews weren't allowed to take their money with them and Edward made sure it all went into his pocket. He did it for the money but it made him popular as well. Aaron told my father how the Jews were hissed and spat at in the streets. They were hated, especially in Lincoln where a little choir boy was supposed to have been murdered by Jews on his way home from church. You don't hear that story so much now that the Jews have gone. The Italian merchants are the money lenders now, and they'll soon be as unpopular as the Jews were.

I also need to equip my son Andrew for the wars in France. He'll need new armour. It's no

good using mine. It won't fit and that's dangerous. If your helmet slips over your eyes because it's too big – well, that may be the death of you.

It takes me back to when I was young, off to join the first King Edward in his wars against the Scots. 'The Hammer of the Scots' we called him but those days of glory have gone. It was a day of shame when his son, the second Edward, lost the Battle of Bannockburn to the Scots. He's dead now, God rest his soul, and our new young king looks like taking after his grandfather. Andrew dreams of being knighted on the battlefield – just what a young man should dream of.

This is where we part. Tomorrow I'll travel north to our lands in Yorkshire with all the family and servants. It's a lot for the steward to organise but I trust him. We'll need wine, spices, clothes, tapestries for the walls, not to mention a few barrels of silver pennies. And there's shields, swords and bows – we can't travel unarmed. There must be close on fifty people travelling when we move from one estate to another. I hope our steward in Yorkshire is ready to feed us all!

Farewell, travellers, and good fortune!

◆ The Luttrell Psalter

Sir Geoffrey Luttrell *did* have that book of prayers made for him. It is called the Luttrell Psalter. A psalter is a book of prayers and psalms. It still exists today and the pictures here are taken from it. The pictures tell us a great deal about life in the 1300s because they show real scenes and people from the village of Irnham in Lincolnshire. (In the Middle Ages it was called Gerneham but the name changed later.)

Back-breaking work for the villagers.

Dinner in the hall. Sir Geoffrey is in the centre.

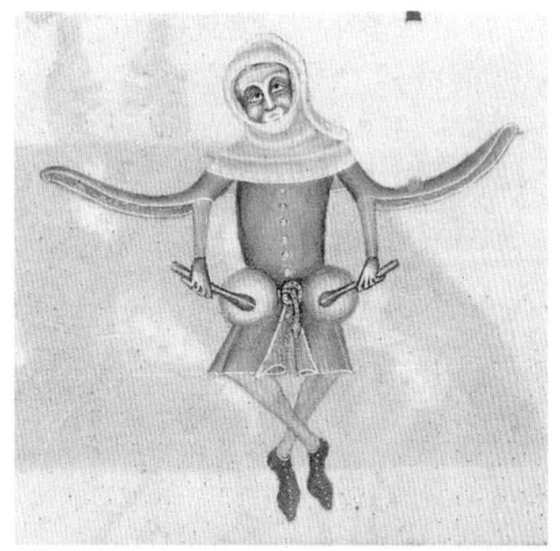

A musician.

A ploughman with his oxen.

Preparing a meal for the Luttrells. The people shown in the picture may be William, John and other servants mentioned in Sir Geoffrey's will.

Sir Geoffrey Luttrell with Lady Agnes. The other woman is probably Beatrice, their daughter-in-law.

Bear-baiting.

Real lives

Key

Danger

We know quite a lot about the Luttrell family. The Luttrells were rich landowners and so we can find out when they were born and died from government records. Sir Geoffrey's will also still exists and that tells us about some of his servants as well as about his family.

The stories you have read are set in 1330. **Sir Geoffrey** and **Lady Agnes** continued to live at Irnham and their other estates in Yorkshire and Nottingham. Their son, **Andrew**, did go off to fight in Edward III's wars against France and their youngest daughter, **Isabel**, did become a nun.

In 1340 Lady Agnes died, aged about 57, and Sir Geoffrey died five years later, aged 69, and was buried at Irnham. In his will he left the huge sum of £200 to be given to the poor in the month after his death, and another £20 for wine, food and spices for the gathering of family and friends after his burial. Sir Geoffrey also left money to **Joan, the Lady's Maid**, to **Alice, the Chambermaid**, to about ten other servants including **John, the cook**, and to his five godchildren, who were all children of his servants.

Andrew inherited his father's lands. He and **Beatrice** had no children. She went on a pilgrimage abroad in 1350, perhaps to Spain. We don't know when she died but we know that she was dead by 1363 because that was the year Andrew married his second wife, **Hawisia**, who was aged 18. Their son was born soon afterwards.

Andrew died in 1390, aged 77, and you can still see the brass carving made in his memory in Irnham church.

Another sack of grain for the miller.

A boy climbing a cherry tree.

◆ Could you live in 1330?

It's time for your first important decision. These pages will help you to decide whether you would like to live in 1330. The information here sums up life in Irnham in 1330 and the Activities will help you to think carefully about your decision.

Life was hard for most people. There were about five million people in England then. It was difficult to grow enough food for everyone.

Poor diet explains why so many babies and children died. Many mothers also died while giving birth, or soon afterwards from **infection**. Even the smallest cut could lead to death from blood poisoning. If you lived to 20 then, on average, you could expect to live until you were 40. The Luttrells lived longer, but they were lucky and were helped by a better diet.

Death was never far away. This made **religion** very important. Life on earth was harsh so people looked forward to Heaven. Another reason was that the only holidays were holy days when the church was the centre of celebrations. Everyone went to the same church because there was only one kind of Christianity in Britain – the Catholic Church led by the Pope in Rome.

Work was different for cottagers, villeins and freemen. About 40 per cent of people were villeins. Many lords had freed some of their villeins. It was cheaper to employ freemen just for the times they were needed and at low wages. However, they did not want to set everyone free and so villeins had little chance to improve their lives. To do that they needed freedom, plenty of work and higher wages. Most were keen to improve the way they lived. After all, they were just as intelligent as us, even if they weren't taught to read and write.

Freemen – farmers or men like the miller. They owned or rented land. They worked for the lord for wages. They could grow wealthier if they worked hard and bought more land.

Villeins – farmers or servants. They and their families belonged to the lord. So did all their animals and land. In return for their land they had to work on the lord's land, the demesne, for two or three days each week.

Cottagers – they got no land from the lord so they had to find work for wages when they could. They had a little land around their cottages, often the poorest land for growing food. They suffered most when work and food were scarce.

Perhaps you were unlucky to land in 1330. Life wasn't the same throughout the Middle Ages. Between 1000 and 1300 the weather was warmer, harvests were better and people were wealthier, with more food and work to go round. That's when many of the great cathedrals, like the one in Lincoln, were being built. The money to build them came from the profits from farming. A hundred years later, in 1430, you would have lived far more comfortably than in 1330 – but that's a story for later.

Key

Comfort

Work

Enjoyment

Danger

Freedom

ACTIVITY A

Whom would you most like to be in Irnham?

Choose the person in Irnham whom you would most like to be. Write a paragraph explaining your choice. You could use these sentence starters to help you plan your paragraph.

The person I would most like to be is . . .

One reason for this is that . . .

Another reason is . . .

Finally, the most important reason I would like to be him or her is . . .

ACTIVITY B

Whom would you least like to be?

Choose the person in Irnham whom you would least like to be. Write a paragraph explaining your choice. You could use the same pattern for your paragraph as the one given in Activity A.

ACTIVITY C

1 a) Draw your own copy of the chart below. Fill in the columns with reasons supporting each statement. You should have plenty to work with from your sorting grid. Include things you would miss about life today as well as things, good or bad, about 1330.

I would prefer to live in 1330 rather than today because . . .	I do not want to live in 1330 but I could put up with it because . . .	I would hate to live in 1330 because . . .

b) Put a star against the three reasons that are most important in helping you to decide whether you want to live in 1330. They can all be in one column or in different columns.

2 Draw your own copy of the pendulum on page 4. Draw the arrow on your pendulum to show your decision about whether you would like to live in 1330.

3 Explain your decision. You could write paragraphs explaining the reasons for living in 1330, the reasons against living in 1330, and which reason was most important in reaching your decision. You can get a sheet from your teacher to help you with this task.

ACTIVITY D

It's time to leave 1330. But before you can travel forward in time, you need to stock up with food, drink and fuel for the journey. Find:

a) three types of food and one of drink from Sir Geoffrey's table

b) one type of food and one of drink from Heloise, wife of Piers the villein

c) one kind of fuel.

Have you got the things you need? Right, fasten your seat belts and good luck, whenever you land.

1.3 A PEEP AT PEPYS

Meet Samuel

6 January. Up, leaving my wife and the maids to get supper for our company. I to Whitehall and my business, then home to dinner and did then take coach to the Duke's theatre with Mr Harris, my wife, her maid and three friends, which did cost me 20 shillings besides oranges. After the play, stayed till Harris was dressed (he having acted in 'The Tempest') and so all by coaches home, where we find my house with good fires and candles ready, and a company of friends and neighbours.

And so with much pleasure we to dancing, having the Duke of Buckingham's musicians, the best in town. By and by to a very good supper, and mighty merry and good music playing; and after supper to dancing and singing till about twelve at night; and then we had a good wine and an excellent cake, cost me near 20 shillings of our Jane's making, which was cut into twenty pieces, there being by this time so many of our company. And so to dancing again and singing with extraordinary great pleasure, till about two in the morning; and so away to bed, weary and mightily pleased.

Key

Comfort

Enjoyment

ACTIVITY

This could be your home – for ever.

1 What century or period do you think this is? Think about the periods you have studied before. Is this closest to the Romans, the Saxons and Vikings, the Tudors, the Victorians?
2 Which details from the diary or the picture give you the best clues about the date?
3 Compare this scene with life in Irnham in 1330. In what ways is it:
   a) similar
   b) different?
4 You will need to decide whether you can live here. As you explore, fill in your sorting grid with as much information as you can find.

◆ Murder and robbery

Samuel

My name is Samuel Pepys. Blessed be God I find myself worth above £6200, having four maids and one man-servant, this year of 1666. This day to the coffee house where I heard Colonel Baron tell good stories of his travels in Asia. Also heard tell of a murder in King Street where there was a great stop of coaches and so a falling-out in which a cart driver killed a coachman…

Such stories do make me fear murder and robbery here in London. One day I waked with a noise as if it were breaking down a window and then removing stools and chairs and going up and down our stairs. My wife and I did both conclude that thieves were in the house. I put on my gown and BREECHES and, with a firebrand in my hand, went down and opened my chamber where all was well. Then to the kitchen and found nothing but heard a noise in the chimneys next door and the noise was their chimneys being swept and nothing else.

Another night, THE CONSTABLE AND THE WATCH found our backyard door open and so came in to see what the matter was, but all was well.

When the watch catch thieves, which is not often, the thieves are hanged. There were twelve or fourteen thousand people to see Turner hang for stealing over £4000. I paid a shilling to stand on the wheel of a cart to watch, Turner delaying the time by long prayers in hopes of reprieve but at last he was flung off the ladder.

There are other common entertainments. One day I did go to Shoe Lane to see cock fighting. But Lord, to see the strange variety of people, from Parliament-men to the poorest bakers, brewers and whatnot, all swearing, cursing and betting. I soon had enough of it. It is a very rude and nasty pleasure, like the Bear Garden where I saw the bull's tossing of the dogs. Tomorrow the King and Duke of York set out for Newmarket to some horse races but I to church.

To church

Lord's Day. Up and spent the morning reading in my chamber till the barber came and, being trimmed, to church, myself, wife and servants. Home to dinner, then to church again, where a bawling young Scot preached. During the service I did think on my booksellers. One day I did sit there two or three hours, calling for twenty books to lay my money out upon and found myself at a great loss whether to choose a History of London or Shakespeare's plays, or others. I thank the Lord that I did study at school Latin, Greek, Hebrew, arithmetic, geometry, astronomy and music, for music is the thing of the world that I love most.

I also thought on the fine experiments at the Royal Society of Sciences. I heard Mr Hooke read a lecture about the comet, proving very probably that this is the very same comet that appeared before in the year 1618, and that probably it will appear again. Mr Spong did bring a lantern with pictures in glass to make strange things appear on a wall, very pretty. We did also at night see Jupiter very fine with my 12 foot glass, but could not see Saturn, he being very dark. Mr Evelyn did show me letters in the very handwriting of Queen Elizabeth and Queen Mary of Scots, but Lord, how poorly methinks they wrote in those days.

So home after church to reading and supper and after some pleasant talk, my wife and I to prayers and to bed. Myself somewhat vexed at my wife's neglect in leaving her scarf and waistcoat in the coach, though I confess she did give them to me to look after. It was her fault not to see that I did not take them out of the coach.

Key

Enjoyment

Danger

◆ Women's work

Elizabeth

So Samuel is angry with me because he lost my scarf? That is just like Samuel. Let me tell you about the last time we had friends home for dinner. I rose by five o'clock in the morning, and went to market. I had for them oysters; then at first course, rabbits, lamb and beef; next, a great dish of roasted fowl and a tart; and then fruit and cheese. I had our house mighty clean and neat, with good fires in our dining room, Samuel's chamber and my chamber also. At supper we had a good wine and cold meat, and sent our guests away about ten at night. So I, weary, to bed after all my work and organising the servants, and then Samuel said that he was pleased with the way HE had organised dinner for HIS guests!

Sometimes we quarrel mightily. While he is gadding abroad the town, looking after beauties, to put it plainly, I stay lonely at home. I had to plead and argue with Samuel many times before he would pay for a lady to keep me company, or for drawing lessons, or singing and dancing lessons. He is greatly jealous of Mr Pembleton, my dancing master, and finds fault with me if there is money missing when he checks my accounts. One night I gave him some cross answer, and he did strike me over my left eye such a blow as I did cry out and was in great pain; but yet my spirit was such as to bite and scratch him. Presently we were friends and Samuel was sorry to think what he had done, but my eye was black which scared him because the servants would know what had happened.

We are happy together despite all this. He said how pleased he was when I chose him as my valentine this year. He also did buy me a pearl necklace and diamond ring and did give me £30 a year for all my expenses, including clothes, which was more than I expected. He also paid £20 for clothes for me for Easter. He did boggle mightily at the parting with his money but at last did give it to me.

I do keep his house clean. Washday is the longest day. I and my maids are up before dawn and at work all day, sometimes past one o'clock at night till all is done. Samuel treats the servants well as long as they do their work. But he can be harsh with them if they do wrong. Once, coming home, he saw our door left open by Lucy, our cookmaid. This so vexed him that he did give her a kick and offered a blow at her. But he is kind too. When Jane, who had been with us ten years, married Tom Edwards, who works in Samuel's office, Samuel gave them £80 as a wedding present.

Samuel does not like me to be away from home. He does say that home is all melancholy when I am not there so I keep him company on his travels. One summer we travelled in our coach to Bristol. On the way we paid a guide to take us to Stonehenge which was as huge as I had been told and worth going this journey to see. God knows what its use was. You can hire a hammer from a blacksmith for a penny, to take pieces off the stones, but we did not. We visited Bath and saw the baths with all the people in them. I think it cannot be clean to have so many bodies together in the same water. Soon, I hope, we will take ourselves to France and travel around as a holiday now that Samuel is worth so much money.

Key

Comfort

Work

Enjoyment

Freedom

Lord, have mercy upon us

Samuel

My wife dreams of travels to France where her family did come from. I confess I do not like to leave London. Once, when I visited my uncle and aunt near Cambridge, I had a terrible journey, along DYKES where sometimes my horse sank to the belly. I found my uncle and aunt and their daughters, poor wretches, in a sad poor thatched cottage, like a poor barn or stable, and in a poor condition of habit; took them to a miserable inn and set down to supper. By and by news was brought that one of our horses was stolen out of the stable. I went to bed in a sad, cold, nasty chamber and so to sleep till the morning but was bit by the gnats.

London is busy, rich and full of life, although you would not think it to listen to my wife. She says she is unhappy and lonely at home but does not seem so when her dancing master does visit her, sometimes twice a day. I confess myself deadly full jealous and do listen to see if they are really dancing or no. Yet we are happy enough, and glad to be alive. I remember well the day in 1665 when I did see two or three houses marked with a red cross upon the doors and 'Lord, have mercy upon us' writ there. Soon 3000 were dead of the plague each week and how sad a sight it was to see the streets empty of people and two shops in three shut up. Every day, sadder and sadder news of the increase of plague. In the city died, one week in August, 6102 of the plague. Lord, what a sad time it was, to see no boats on the river and grass grow all up and down Whitehall and nobody but poor wretches in the streets.

I was too busy to leave my work even in the worst days of plague, and now even busier. We are at war with the Dutch and their ships raid our towns. Yesterday to the Duke of York, who declared we have no more money for building new ships nor for supplies and weapons. Returned to the office, shutting the doors that I and my clerks might not be interrupted. So, with only a little dinner, we were very busy all the day until about ten at night. To bed about three hours and then waked, troubling myself about the navy till, about six o'clock, at last got my wife to talk to comfort me.

Most grieved by the shipping of the PRESSED MEN. Lord, how some poor women did cry and run from one group of men to another, looking for their husbands and weeping over every ship that set sail and watching it as far as they could by moonlight. Besides, to see honest labouring men and husbands, leaving poor wives and families, taken suddenly by the press-gang, was very hard, but we have no money to pay sailors so must press men where we cannot recruit them willingly.

This morning I was let blood, and did bleed about 14 ounces, towards curing my eyes which are sore as soon as candle-light comes to them. Dr Turberville did give me pills and green lenses as well as bleeding, but the best remedy is my Tube-spectacle, a narrow tube of paper stopping the glare of the candle paining my eyes. One day I went with Turberville and other doctors to dissect eyes of sheep and oxen, but strange that Turberville to this day has seen no human eyes dissected but just once.

In all other ways I am in good health, though I am at a great loss to know whether it be wearing my hare's foot or taking every morning a pill of turpentine. I must thank God for my good fortune. In 1661 I was worth but £300, but now find my worth to be over £6000. Thus ends my journal, I being not able to do it any longer from fear of blindness, my eyes so sore from overworking them.

◆ Samuel Pepys and his diary

Samuel and **Elizabeth Pepys** went on their travels to France and also to Holland, but their holiday ended in tragedy. Elizabeth fell ill. She travelled home but died three weeks later, aged 29. They had been married for fourteen years. They were usually happy together but they did have fierce quarrels. Samuel was very jealous of any man Elizabeth spoke to, and especially of the dancing master he employed to teach her. Strangely, he never mentioned Elizabeth by name in his diary, and did not mention her birthdays, although he did once note that he had forgotten their anniversary.

Samuel did not marry again, although he was only 36 when Elizabeth died. He became richer and more important, building up and organising the Royal Navy so that it became the most powerful navy in Europe. He also became a Member of Parliament. Happily, he was wrong about his eyes: he never did go blind. When he died, aged 70, in 1703, he was buried next to Elizabeth in St Olave's Church, London. As you can see from the family tree on the opposite page, he was fortunate to live so long. Most of his brothers and sisters died at a much younger age than him.

Jane Birch and **Tom Edwards** were servants in the Pepys house for many years. Jane started work for them in 1658 and Tom began to work for Samuel in 1664. Tom and Jane married in 1669. Pepys gave them £80 as a wedding present. They had two children. The elder was named **Samuel** and became an officer in the Royal Navy.

The diary

Pepys kept his diary from 1660 to 1669 and often wrote three or four pages a day. It was written in shorthand for speed. The diary is one of the most important sources of evidence of life in the 1660s. Everything you read on pages 26–33 is taken from Pepys' diary, although entries from different dates have been put together to give you as much information about his life as possible. Elizabeth did not keep a diary. The words she speaks on pages 30–31 are taken from Samuel's diary but have been turned round to give her side of the story.

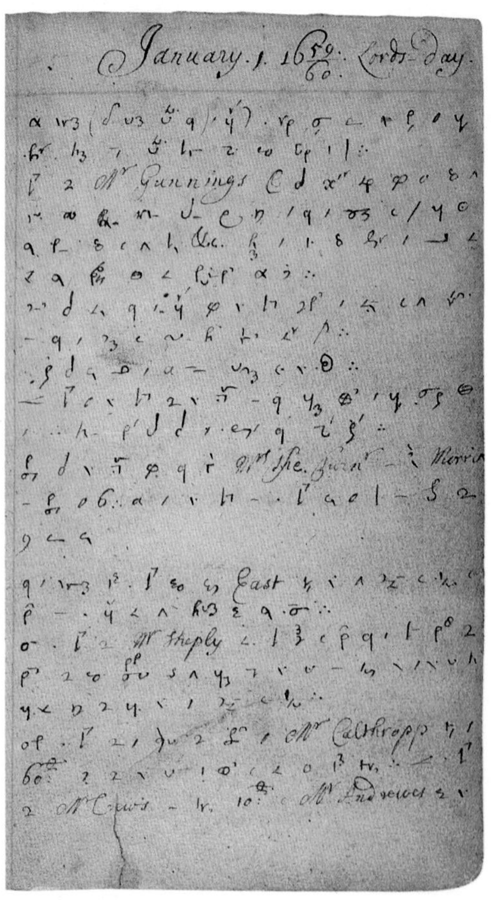

SOURCE 1 The opening page of Pepys' diary. This is the entry for 1 January 1660 – Lord's Day (see page 29).

SOURCES 2A and 2B These pictures of Samuel and Elizabeth Pepys were painted in 1666 by Hailes. Pepys wrote in his diary that he was 'mightily pleased with my wife's picture'. Samuel is holding a piece of music that he composed himself.

SOURCE 3 Samuel Pepys' family tree, showing the age at death.

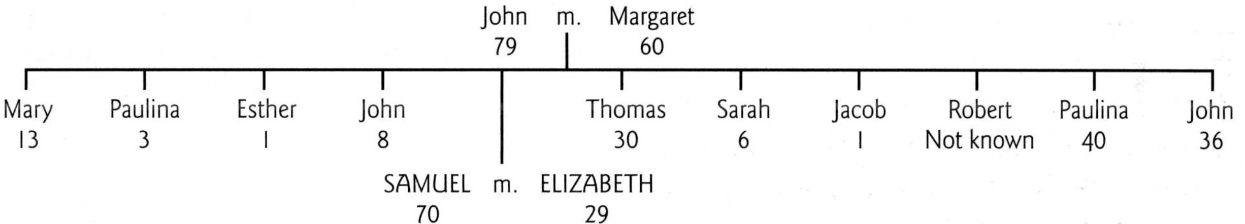

Health and disease

The Pepys family was typical. Several children died as babies or toddlers but some members of the family lived long lives. Samuel was lucky. When he was only 25 he survived an operation without an anaesthetic that could easily have killed him. He had been suffering from a terrible pain, caused by a stone in his bladder. The pain became so bad that sometimes he could not stop himself crying out. He decided that he had to risk surgery. Samuel was probably tied down and then the surgeon made a three-inch cut, deep enough to reach in and take out the stone. It weighed two ounces and was as big as a tennis ball. Later that year the surgeon did the same operation on four more people but they all died. He used new instruments that were free from infection on Samuel, but later they became infected and so passed on the infection from patient to patient. In the 1660s surgeons did not know that germs caused disease and there were no antibiotics or antiseptics to kill infections.

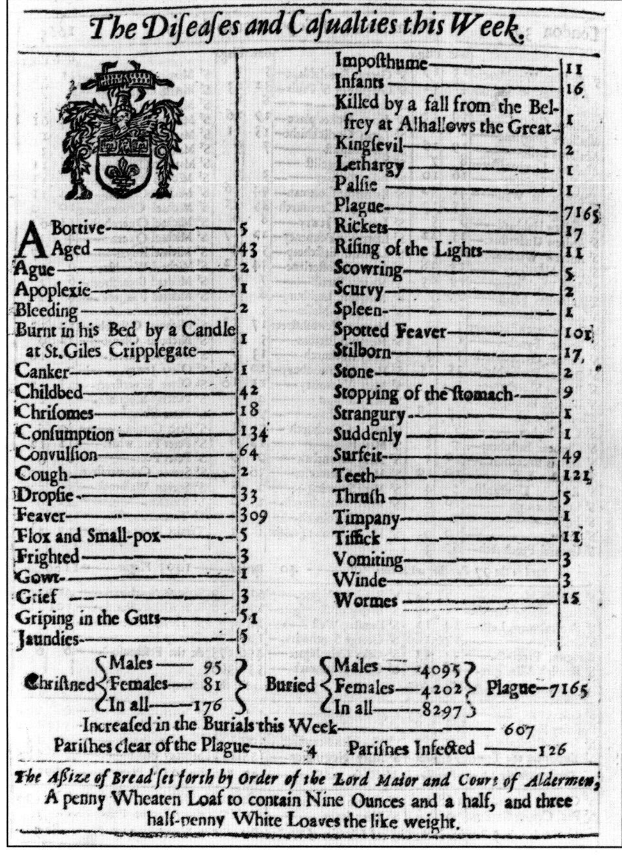

The Diſeaſes and Caſualties this Week.

Abortive	5	Impoſthume	11
Aged	43	Infants	16
Ague	2	Killed by a fall from the Belfrey at Alhallows the Great	1
Apoplexie	1	Kingſevil	2
Bleeding	2	Lethargy	1
Burnt in his Bed by a Candle at St. Giles Cripplegate	1	Palſie	1
Canker	1	Plague	7165
Childbed	42	Rickets	17
Chriſomes	18	Riſing of the Lights	11
Conſumption	134	Scowring	5
Convulſion	64	Scurvy	2
Cough	2	Spleen	1
Dropſie	33	Spotted Feaver	101
Feaver	309	Stilborn	17
Flox and Small-pox	5	Stone	2
Frighted	3	Stopping of the ſtomach	9
Gowt	1	Strangury	1
Grief	3	Suddenly	1
Griping in the Guts	51	Surfeit	49
Jaundies	5	Teeth	121
		Thruſh	5
		Timpany	1
		Tiffick	11
		Vomiting	3
		Winde	3
		Wormes	15

Chriſtned: Males 95, Females 81, In all 176
Buried: Males 4095, Females 4202, In all 8297 — Plague 7165
Increaſed in the Burials this Week — 607
Pariſhes clear of the Plague — 4 Pariſhes Infected — 126

The Aſsize of Bread ſet forth by Order of the Lord Maior and Court of Aldermen;
A penny Wheaten Loaf to contain Nine Ounces and a half, and three half-penny White Loaves the like weight.

SOURCE 4 A mortality bill from 1665. It shows all the causes of death in London during one week.

Stowaway in time – Sir Geoffrey visits the 1660s!

Did you spot a familiar face on page 30? When you travelled through time from 1330 you had a stowaway on board – Sir Geoffrey Luttrell. Sir Geoffrey has lots of questions to ask Samuel and Elizabeth Pepys.

ACTIVITY

As you read through pages 36–42 you will find a lot more information to add to your sorting grid.

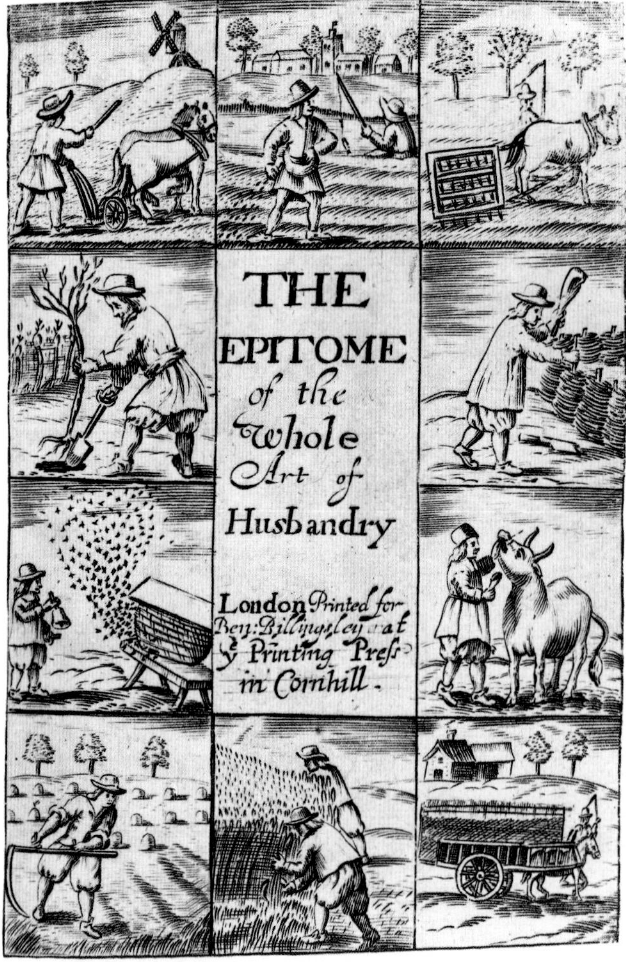

SOURCE 5 Farming scenes from the 1600s, shown on the cover of a book. Most people in England at this time worked on the land.

TOWN AND COUNTRY

Sir Geoffrey Luttrell: *London is so big and there are so many people. Does everyone in England live here?*

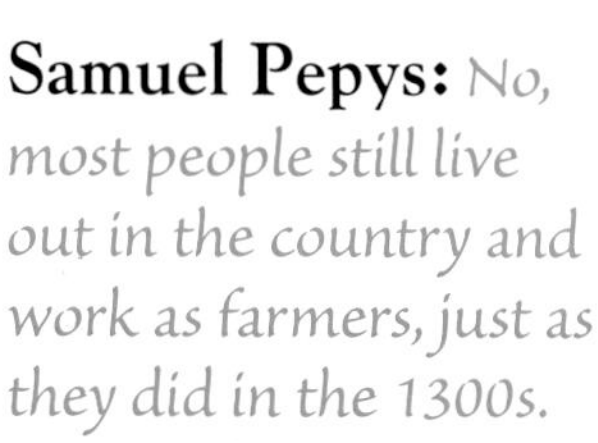

Samuel Pepys: *No, most people still live out in the country and work as farmers, just as they did in the 1300s. Oxen or horses still pull the ploughs and everything else is done by hand. We still depend on the harvest for our food. If there's a good harvest then there is enough food for everyone and prices fall. If the weather is poor and there's a bad harvest, then food prices go up because there isn't enough food to go round. In the worst years, people starve. We import some food from abroad, but not enough to save the poor from starvation. My poor aunt and uncle, who I told you about on page 32, sometimes find it difficult to make ends meet because of the harvest.*

VILLEINS AND FREEMEN

Sir Geoffrey Luttrell: *It's good to hear that farming is still so important. The villeins must be hard at work in the fields.*

Samuel Pepys: *That's one thing that has changed. There are no villeins now. Every man is free to travel and work where he likes. People work for money. If the son of a poor man works hard and is clever then he can become rich and powerful. That's much easier than it was.*

WOMEN

Sir Geoffrey Luttrell: *Are women free to do whatever they like, too?*

Samuel Pepys: *Women are still supposed to obey their fathers or husbands in everything. Many do, but some take charge of their own lives. Some work as actresses. Until recently, boys played women's roles in plays.*

Elizabeth Pepys: *Men are frightened by women thinking for themselves. Look at this booklet, written to show the dangers of allowing women to be equal to men. Dangers! There is no danger in women thinking for themselves.*

Sir Geoffrey Luttrell: *No villeins; women thinking for themselves! It sounds as if the world has turned upside down since my day.*

THE 220

Parliament of VVomen.

With the merrie Lawes by them newly Enacted. To live in more Eaſe, Pompe, Pride, and wantonneſſe: but eſpecially that they might have ſuperiority and domineere over their husbands; with a new way found out by them to cure any old or new Cuckolds, and how both parties may recover their credit and honeſty againe

London, Printed for W.Wilſon and are to be ſold by him in Will-yard in Little Saint Bartholomewes. 1646.

Aug: 14 - London 1646

SOURCE 6 A pamphlet from 1649 making fun of women wanting equality with men.

THE CIVIL WAR

Samuel Pepys: *It has! When I was growing up there was Civil War in Britain. Parliament fought against King Charles I. The King said that he could rule the country and raise taxes however he liked, without asking Parliament for advice. Parliament said that he had to rule with its advice and help. They couldn't agree so there was Civil War for seven years, from 1642 until 1649.*

Elizabeth Pepys: *The Civil War caused a lot of damage and fear. Over 100,000 people were killed in the fighting and many more died of diseases spread during sieges and through armies. They say 20 per cent of the population died during the years of the Civil War. Houses were destroyed in at least 150 towns. After the siege of Taunton there were heaps of rubbish, ruined houses in their own ashes, here a chimney, there a little fragment of wall.*

Samuel Pepys: *The war only ended when Charles I was executed.*

Sir Geoffrey Luttrell: *So you don't have a king any more?*

Samuel Pepys: *We had eleven years without a king but no one could decide how to govern the country. They even asked Oliver Cromwell, the army leader, to be king.*

SOURCE 7 The execution of King Charles I, 1649.

PARLIAMENT

Sir Geoffrey Luttrell: *King Cromwell?*

Samuel Pepys: *No. He refused! I still think Cromwell was a good man but not many people dare agree with me these days. People only remember that his Puritans tried to stop people enjoying themselves; they closed the theatres and put an end to Christmas. They failed, but I think Cromwell always tried to do his best for the country.*

Sir Geoffrey Luttrell: *So you don't have a king at all now?*

Samuel Pepys: *In the end Parliament asked Charles I's son to come back as King so we have a king once again. But Parliament is much more powerful now than in the 1300s. The King has to listen to what Parliament wants.*

Sir Geoffrey Luttrell: *Who controls Parliament, now it is so important?*

Samuel Pepys: *Parliament is still full of rich landowners. In the 1640s some people called Levellers wanted every man to have a vote but Cromwell stopped that nonsense. Ordinary people can't vote in elections for Members of Parliament unless they own quite a lot of land. No women, however rich, are allowed to vote.*

SOURCE 8 Oliver Cromwell, Lord Protector of England, 1653–1658.

RELIGION

Sir Geoffrey Luttrell: *I'll tell you who I haven't seen. I haven't seen any monks.*

Samuel Pepys: *No, that's another great change – religion. Until the 1530s everyone belonged to the Catholic Church. The monasteries were very rich. Then Henry VIII set up the Church of England in the 1530s and closed down all the monasteries. He did not want the monks obeying the Pope instead of him as king.*

Elizabeth Pepys: *And he wanted all the wealth belonging to the monasteries!*

SOURCE 9 A painting showing soldiers ransacking a monastery.

A MAP OF THE WORLD

Samuel Pepys: *Catholics and other Christians who are not part of the Church of England are second-class citizens. They're not allowed to vote in elections or become Members of Parliament. Some have emigrated to America so that they can worship God in their own way.*

Sir Geoffrey Luttrell: *America? Where's that?*

Samuel Pepys: *It's far away from here. We've discovered lots of new countries since your day. Our sailors have sailed all the way round the world.*

Sir Geoffrey Luttrell: *Didn't they fall off the edge?*

Elizabeth Pepys: *The world is round – everyone knows that!*

Samuel Pepys: *America is where my pipe tobacco comes from.*

Sir Geoffrey Luttrell: *Strange habit! I'm glad they didn't smoke in my day.*

Elizabeth Pepys: *Look at this globe. That's Africa, where our black cookmaid Doll comes from. It's very fashionable to have a black servant these days.*

Sir Geoffrey Luttrell: *I've seen a lot of black people here.*

Samuel Pepys: *Most of them are slaves. English traders buy slaves in Africa then sell them in the West Indies and America … A few of them also come to England.*

WEAPONS

Sir Geoffrey Luttrell: *My men fought with swords and longbows. What kind of weapons do you use today?*

Samuel Pepys: *Our soldiers use swords but guns and gunpowder are much more powerful.*

SOURCE 10 By the 1660s educated people had quite an accurate map of most of the world.

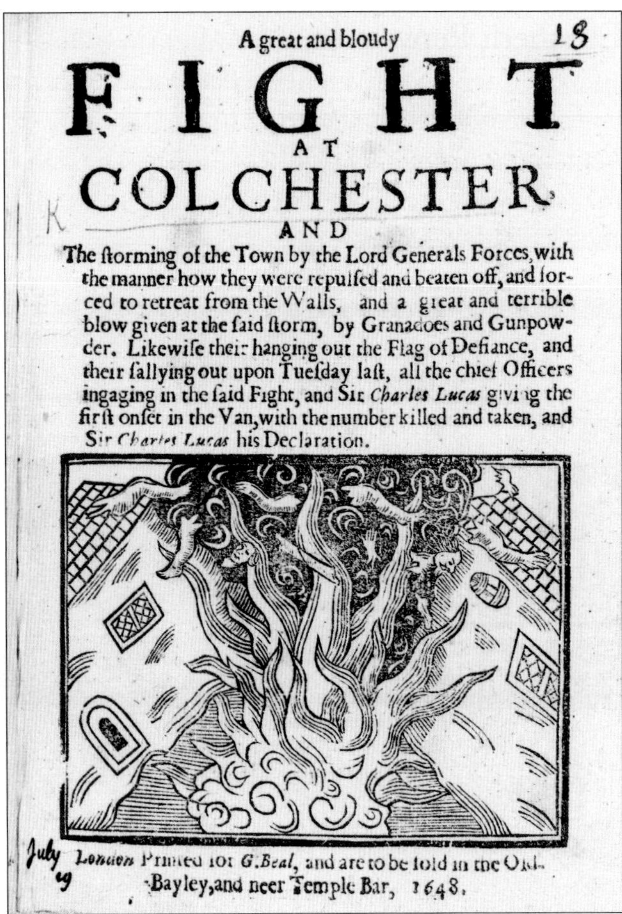

A great and bloudy

FIGHT

AT

COLCHESTER

AND

The ſtorming of the Town by the Lord Generals Forces, with the manner how they were repulſed and beaten off, and forced to retreat from the Walls, and a great and terrible blow given at the ſaid ſtorm, by Granadoes and Gunpowder. Likewiſe their hanging out the Flag of Defiance, and their ſallying out upon Tueſday laſt, all the chief Officers ingaging in the ſaid Fight, and Sir *Charles Lucas* giving the firſt onſet in the Van, with the number killed and taken, and Sir *Charles Lucas* his Declaration.

London Printed for *G.Beal*, and are to be ſold in the Old-Bayley, and neer Temple Bar, 1648.

SOURCE 11 A pamphlet showing the results of a mortar grenade at the Siege of Colchester during the Civil War.

HOUSES AND FURNITURE

Sir Geoffrey Luttrell: *Lots of the houses in London seem very new.*

Samuel Pepys: *That's because thousands of churches and homes were rebuilt after the Great Fire in 1666. Stone and brick are much safer than timber, especially as we still use candles for light and have wood or coal fires.*

Sir Geoffrey Luttrell: *There's lots of new things in your house. You have a fireplace and chimney to take away the smoke; glass windows instead of wooden shutters; and you have curtains. The feather mattresses on the beds look more comfortable than straw, and it seems that most people have tin or pewter plates and spoons instead of wooden bowls. These forks are very useful too – when were they invented?*

Elizabeth Pepys: *I don't know but I'm glad we've got new foods: you never had potatoes, tea, coffee or chocolate. Meat and fish are still the main foods if you have plenty of money. The poor make do with vegetables, bread and ale, just as they have always done.*

SOURCE 12a A London town house in about 1650.

SOURCE 12b The Great Fire of London in 1666 destroyed most of the centre of London. This was because most of the buildings were made of wood, like those in Source 12a. After the fire, London was rebuilt using stone. The most famous new building was St Paul's Cathedral, designed by Sir Christopher Wren.

SEWAGE

Sir Geoffrey Luttrell: *Hah, I see that one thing in life hasn't changed!*

Samuel Pepys: *No, our servants still empty the chamber pots into cess pits. Then the cess pits are emptied by night-soil men who cart the waste into the countryside. We send the servants to collect our fresh water from pipes or streams.*

SOURCE 13 A seventeenth-century chamber pot.

BOOKS AND EDUCATION

Sir Geoffrey Luttrell: *You have many books. Do you have a psalter like mine?*

Samuel Pepys: *Your psalter was written by hand. My books are all printed. Printing is another great revolution. Books have spread ideas all over Europe and led to all kinds of scientific discoveries.*

Sir Geoffrey Luttrell: *Can everybody read these days? Hardly anybody could read in my day.*

Samuel Pepys: *Many children learn their letters from horn books. Literacy is important for getting better work. In the country as a whole nearly 40 per cent of men can read – in London it's nearly 80 per cent. Far fewer women can read, but then it's more important to teach girls to frisk and dance, paint their faces and curl their hair.*

Elizabeth Pepys: *Ha!*

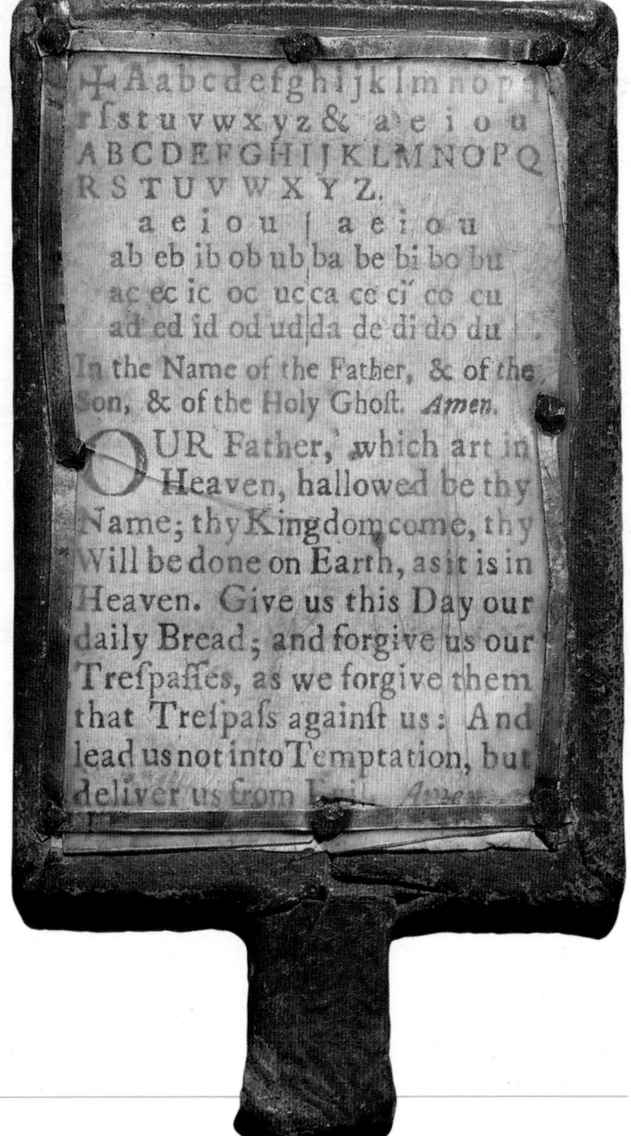

SOURCE 14 A horn book.

CRIME AND PUNISHMENT

Sir Geoffrey Luttrell: *What's happening in this picture?*

Elizabeth Pepys: *It's from a book about witches. This woman's being 'swum' to see if she's a witch. If she sinks under the water she's innocent. If she floats she's guilty, because the Devil must be saving her from drowning. There are lots of books about witches. You should read one.*

Sir Geoffrey Luttrell: *Is that how you punish all criminals?*

Samuel Pepys: *No, only witches. Most crimes are thefts and thieves are hanged, but we don't catch many criminals. The watchmen and constables only go on watch when they've finished their normal jobs.*

SOURCE 15

An illustration from the front page of a pamphlet describing how to decide whether a woman 'be a witch or not'.

HEALTH

Sir Geoffrey Luttrell: *I'll tell you another thing that hasn't changed – sickness. I've seen many sick people in your streets. Babies and children still die young and many mothers die giving birth. And you still use herbal remedies to cure illnesses. My wife, Lady Agnes, uses many of the same cures.*

Samuel Pepys: *What else is there? We praise God if we live to be 50, what with plague returning year after year. We always watch out for comets – they're a sign of terrible events about to happen.*

Elizabeth Pepys: *We have had enough terrible events for a lifetime – the plague, the Great Fire, and that awful Civil War.*

◆ Could you live in 1669?

It's now time for your second important decision. This page helps you to decide whether you would like to live in 1669.

ACTIVITY A

Would you like to be Samuel Pepys in London in 1669?
Decide whether you would like to swap places with Samuel Pepys. Write a paragraph explaining your choice. You could use the sentence starters below to help you plan your paragraph.

I would/would not like to change places with Samuel Pepys.
One reason for this is that . . .
Another reason is . . .
Finally, the most important reason I would/would not like to be Samuel Pepys is . . .

ACTIVITY B

Would you like to be Elizabeth Pepys?
Decide whether you would like to swap places with Elizabeth Pepys. Write a paragraph explaining your choice. You could use similar sentence starters to those above.

ACTIVITY C

1 a) Draw your own copy of the chart below. Fill in the columns with reasons supporting each statement. Include things you would miss about life today as well as things, good or bad, about 1669.

I would prefer to live in 1669 rather than today because . . .	I do not want to live in 1669 but I could put up with it because . . .	I would hate to live in 1669 because . . .

b) Put a star against the three reasons that are most important in helping you to decide whether you want to live in 1669. They can all be in one column or from different columns.

2 Draw your own copy of the pendulum on page 4. Draw the arrow on your pendulum to show your decision about whether you would like to live in 1669.

3 Explain your decision. Make sure that you include paragraphs on the reasons for living in 1669, the reasons against living in 1669, and which reason was most important in reaching your decision. You can get a sheet from your teacher to help you.

ACTIVITY D

It's time to leave 1669, but before you go you need:

a) three types of food and one of drink from Samuel Pepys' house

b) one kind of fuel.

Have you got all that? OK, fasten your seat belts and good luck, whenever you land.

1.4 LARK RISE TO LONDON

◆ *Laura goes home*

Laura

There! Can you see the village? I'm home at last! It has been good to have your company this last step of the way – I'm tired after walking the eight miles from Candleford. Little traffic passes our village. An occasional farm wagon piled with sacks or hay; a farmer on horseback; a string of horses; and perhaps one of the old penny-farthing bicycles. People rush to their doors to see one of those come past.

This is my village, Lark Rise. There are only about thirty cottages and an inn. The only shop is a small general one in the back kitchen of the inn. The church and school are in the next village which is a mile and a half away.

It is good to be home. It's been seven months since I left to work and live in the Post Office at Candleford. Mother will want to know why I have not been home before. 'Laura,' she'll say, 'you promised to visit every few weeks.' Miss Lane, who runs the Post Office, has offered me the chance to be a postwoman delivering letters. It will be an extra four shillings a week but I need permission from my parents before I can accept. I do hope they'll agree. They may think it a strange job for a woman, let alone a 15-year-old girl.

Can you see the end house, a little apart and turning its back on its neighbours, as though to run away into the fields? That's where my family lives. Look, there's my brother, Edmund, and my sisters – oh, it's so good to see them again!

ACTIVITY

This could be your home – for ever

1. What century or period do you think this is? Think about the periods you have studied before. Is this closest to the Romans, the Saxons and Vikings, the Tudors or the Victorians?
2. Which details give you the best clues about the date?
3. Compare this scene with life in 1669. In what ways is it:
   a) similar
   b) different?
4. You need to decide whether you can live here. As you explore, fill in your sorting grid with as much information as you can find.

Laura's cottage

We don't have beds for visitors, though our house is larger than most. We have two bedrooms but some cottages have only one, divided by a curtain to separate parents and children. Often the big boys sleep downstairs or sleep in another house where the children have already left home. There are no girls older than twelve or thirteen. They are all away, working as servants. As soon as a girl approaches eleven her mother will say, 'About time you were earnin' your livin', me gal!' A girl is made to feel one too many in the overcrowded home, while her brothers work on the farm, bring home a few shillings and are made much of.

Many cottages have just one room downstairs with only a table, a few chairs, some stools and a potato sack thrown down by way of a hearthrug. But they are kept clean by much scrubbing with soap and water. Only three houses in the village have their own water supply. The others get their water from a well or the barrel that every family keeps against the cottage wall to catch rainwater. We use this to wash our clothes and ourselves. The women go to the well in all weathers, carting the buckets home on a YOKE*. The only toilet is in a little bee-hive building at the bottom of the garden. It's just a deep pit with a seat over it. We keep the house door and window shut when it's emptied every six months!*

Every house has a vegetable garden and we have home-grown food in abundance – potatoes, fat green peas, broad beans, cauliflowers a child could use as an armchair, beans, cabbages, lettuces, onions. There's one hot meal a day, bacon, vegetables and a pudding with fruit, currants or jam. For other meals it's usually bread and butter or bread and lard. The men add mustard to theirs and the children get a scraping of black treacle or a sprinkling of brown sugar. Milk is a luxury – it has to be carried a mile and a half from the farm.

Out to work!

Laura

There's plenty of work if you need a job, but you'll have to work hard for your pay. Most men are farmworkers. Before daybreak they throw on their clothes, breakfast on bread and lard and hurry off to the farm. Getting the boys off to work is more difficult. Mothers have to call, push and shake boys of eleven or twelve out of their warm beds. Boys leaving school are taken on at the farm. The farmer says he can always do with extra hands and labour is cheap.

Machinery is just coming into use. At harvest time a THRESHING MACHINE goes from farm to farm and they use a mechanical REAPER, but it does only a small part of the work. Men still mow with scythes and some women are still reaping with sickles. A few women still work in the fields at their own special tasks, weeding and hoeing, picking up stones and topping and tailing turnips. Half a dozen women do this – those who have got their families off their hands and have a longing for a few shillings a week they can call their own.

The farmworkers are paid ten shillings a week but some get paid extra for their special skills. The carter, shepherd, stockman and blacksmith each have two shillings more on their wages and a cottage rent-free. On Friday evenings, when work is done, the men troop up to the farmhouse for their wages, handed out of a window by the farmer himself. He isn't a bad-hearted man and has no idea that he's sweating his workers. 'Don't they get the standard wage and get paid even when there's bad weather? How they live and keep their families on their wages is their own affair. After all, they don't need much, they're not used to luxuries. Besides, don't I give them one good meal a year at my Harvest Home dinner and a joint of beef at Christmas? And soup and milk-puddings for anyone who is ill?'

Key

Work

◆ ... Or to school!

The children start their day almost as early as the farmworkers. School begins at nine o'clock but the children set out as soon as possible after seven o'clock on their mile and a half walk. They like plenty of time to play on the road and their mothers want them out of the way before the clearing up begins. In cold weather some of them carry two hot potatoes to warm their hands, then they eat them for lunch. Although they set off to school early, the children take so much time on the way that the last quarter of a mile is always a race and they rush, panting, into school just as the bell stops. The school is fairly up-to-date although there's no water supply. Instead, rainwater is collected in a small bucket outside.

Reading, writing and arithmetic are the main subjects, with a scripture lesson every morning and needlework every afternoon for the girls. Miss Holmes teaches all the classes in the one room, helped by two monitors who are ex-pupils aged about twelve. History and Geography are not taught separately but there are books, called history 'readers', which contain picturesque stories such as King Alfred and the cakes and Raleigh spreading his cloak before Queen Elizabeth.

Miss Holmes carries a cane, not necessarily to use but as a reminder, for some of the bigger boys get very unruly. She punishes by a smart stroke on each hand but seldom uses the cane on girls, and even more seldom on infants.

Boys of eleven are nearing the end of school. Soon they will be at work and already think of themselves as men. Some parents resent their boys being at school when they could be earning. But others tell them, 'A good education's everything in these days. You can't get on in the world if you ain't had one', for they read the newspapers and new ideas are slowly getting through.

◆ Harvest Home!

Laura

If you stay a few weeks you will still be here for Harvest Home. There aren't many holidays and that's the best of them.

Christmas Day, you see, passes quietly. Mothers with young children buy them an orange each and a handful of nuts, but there's no hanging up of stockings and only those with kind elder sisters or aunts in service get presents.

Still, the farmer gives every man a joint of beef which appears on the Christmas dinner table, with plum pudding – suet duff with a good sprinkling of raisins. Ivy and other evergreens are hung from the ceiling, a bottle of home-made wine is uncorked, and everyone settles down for a kind of super-Sunday. But there are no family reunions because the girls in service cannot be spared from their work and the few boys who have gone out in the world are mostly serving abroad in the Army.

Harvest Home, what a feast it is! The last load of corn is in from the fields. What a bustling in the farmhouse kitchen: such boiling of hams and roasting of beef; such stacking of puddings and baking of loaves. The only ones absent are the bedridden old, and to them portions are carried by the children – slices of beef or ham to the better-off poor; perhaps a ham-bone with plenty of meat left on it to the common poor. My father says the farmer pays starvation wages all year and thinks he makes it up to them with one good meal!

On summer evenings all the children are outdoors. The girls sing game-rhymes like their mothers and grandmothers did, such as 'Oranges and Lemons', 'London Bridge' and 'Here we go round the Mulberry Bush'. The boys play marbles or spin tops, kick an old tin about by way of a football or they climb trees or look for birds' nests. They think nothing of walking five or six miles on a Saturday to play marbles with boys from other villages.

Everybody in the village seems healthy. The open-air life and plenty of simple food must be the reason for it. One old man, nearly 80, has drunk a teacup of frothing soap-suds every Sunday morning for years. 'Them clean the outers,' he says, 'an' stands to reason they must clean the innards too.' Although only babies and small children have baths, the villagers are clean. The women lock their cottage doors for a whole afternoon once a week to have 'a good clean up'. This consists of stripping to the waist and washing downward, then stepping into a footbath and washing upward. We don't have toothbrushes – few people can afford such a luxury – but the women take pride in their strong white teeth and clean them with a scrap of clean, wet rag dipped in salt. Some of the men use soot as tooth-powder.

The old people who have no savings cannot keep their homes after they stop working. Some go to live with their children but there's never room for both: one child takes one parent and another takes the other. If the children can't take them they go to the workhouse. In the workhouse the old couples are separated into the men's and women's buildings. You can imagine the effect of this separation on some faithful old hearts. It's a common thing to hear ageing people say that they hope God takes them before they get past work and become a trouble to anybody.

Over to Candleford

We first went to Candleford one Sunday in the innkeeper's old pony-cart. We found Candleford to be a wonderful town, very large and grand, with a railway station, a doctor's house, lamp-posts, pavements and more people than we had ever seen in our lives before. Instead of having to walk miles just to buy a packet of tea you could dash out without a hat to a shop, or spend whole mornings gazing into shop windows simply stuffed with toys and sweets, furs and watches, and other delightful things. Wages are higher there and the people already had gas to light them to bed and were drawing water out of taps instead of up from a well.

The streets seemed to be full of bicycles. The first penny-farthings were on the roads then, darting and swerving. How fast they travelled and how dangerous they looked. Pedestrians backed almost into hedges when they met one of them, for almost every week there was a story in a newspaper of someone being knocked down and killed by a bicycle. Letters from readers said that cyclists ought not to be allowed to use the roads, which are meant for people to walk on or to drive on with their horses. Bicycles ought to have roads to themselves, like railways.

Nowadays in Candleford I hear the sound of a bugle every Saturday afternoon, followed by the scuffling of dismounting feet as a stream of young men from a cycling club rush into the Post Office to send telegrams. They ride the new low safety bicycle that replaced the penny-farthing. Women ride bicycles too, although the male sex tried hard to keep bicycling for themselves. If a man saw or heard of a woman riding he was horrified. 'Unwomanly. Most unwomanly! God knows what the world's coming to,' he would say, but one woman after another appeared riding a glittering new bicycle. Until then fathers had had all the fun. Now it was their wife's or daughter's turn. The end of the selfish, waited-upon old-fashioned father of the family was sounded by the bicycle bell.

On that first visit to Candleford our cousins came to meet us. Ethel is going to be a teacher, Alma wants to be a dressmaker. Their house seemed like a palace then. When father and Edmund came back from washing their hands, Edmund was bubbling over with a tale of a chain you could pull that brought water pouring down.

After that first visit we went to Candleford more often. That was how I met Miss Lane, an old friend of mother's who keeps the Post Office. Seven months ago Miss Lane sent mother a letter asking if I wanted to start work as a learner at the Post Office, if my parents agreed. That was how I came to leave home in 1890, aged fourteen, and began my adult life at the Post Office. Soon I'll be back there as a postwoman delivering letters. My parents have agreed to my new job. I'm so pleased.

Key

Comfort

Enjoyment

Freedom

◆ Meet Flora Thompson

The last eight pages are taken from *Lark Rise to Candleford*, a book by Flora Thompson. She wrote in the 1930s but she was describing her own childhood in the 1880s. Flora Timms (as she was then) was born in 1876 in the Oxfordshire village of Juniper Hill, the village she called Lark Rise in the book because 'of the great number of skylarks which made the surrounding fields their springboard'.

When she was a child Flora was always asking for paper to write on. This made her mother think that Flora could get a better job than becoming a servant in someone else's house. At the time, around 1890, over 1.5 million people were 'in service' in both wealthy and middle-class homes.

When Flora was a girl she had her fortune told by a gypsy. 'You're going to be loved,' said the fortune teller, 'loved by people you've never seen and never will see.' When Flora's books were published in the 1930s and 1940s they were loved by millions of readers and are still in the shops today.

Flora disguised the real people in her books by changing their names slightly. She called herself Laura, and her brother Edwin became Edmund. Edwin became a soldier when he grew up and served in South Africa. As Flora wrote: 'The boys were expecting to follow the plough all their lives, or, at most, to do a little mild soldiering or go to work in a town. Gallipoli, Ypres, what did they know of such places? But they were to know them, and when the time came they did not flinch. Eleven out of that tiny community never came back again. A brass plate on the wall of the church is engraved with their names (*see below*). A double column, five names long, then, last and alone, the name of Edmund.' Flora's brother was killed in the First World War.

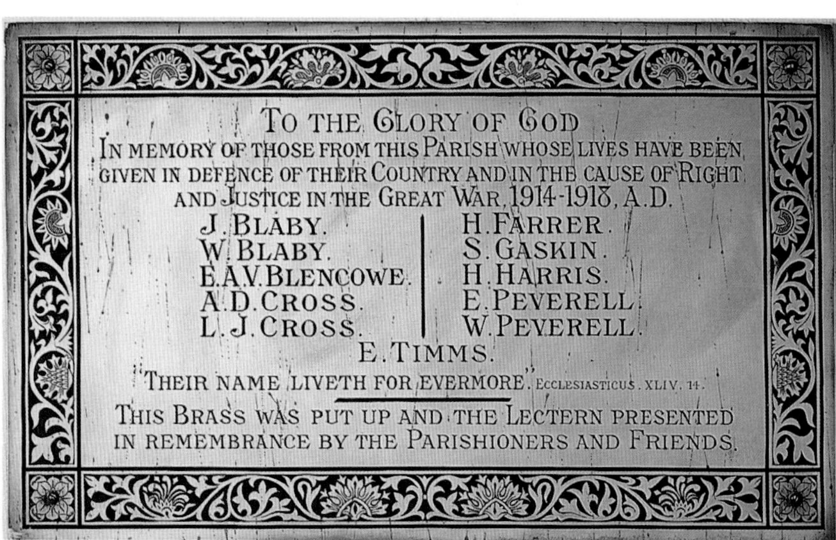

TO THE GLORY OF GOD
IN MEMORY OF THOSE FROM THIS PARISH WHOSE LIVES HAVE BEEN GIVEN IN DEFENCE OF THEIR COUNTRY AND IN THE CAUSE OF RIGHT AND JUSTICE IN THE GREAT WAR, 1914-1918, A.D.
J. BLABY.
W. BLABY.
E.A.V. BLENCOWE.
A.D. CROSS.
L.J. CROSS.
H. FARRER.
S. GASKIN.
H. HARRIS.
E. PEVERELL.
W. PEVERELL.
E. TIMMS.
"THEIR NAME LIVETH FOR EVERMORE." ECCLESIASTICUS. XLIV. 14.
THIS BRASS WAS PUT UP AND THE LECTERN PRESENTED IN REMEMBRANCE BY THE PARISHIONERS AND FRIENDS.

SOURCE I The brass plate commemorating the local men who died in the First World War.

◆ *The stowaways visit London*

Flora's books tell us a lot about life in her village around 1890, but was life the same everywhere in Britain in 1890? Now it's time to use your imagination again. You used your time capsule to visit Flora and Lark Rise but you aren't the only travellers. Remember your stowaway! And this time he's brought a friend!

Sir Geoffrey Luttrell:
These bicycles look fun but nothing else seems to have changed very much. Everybody is still working on farms. I think I could live here.

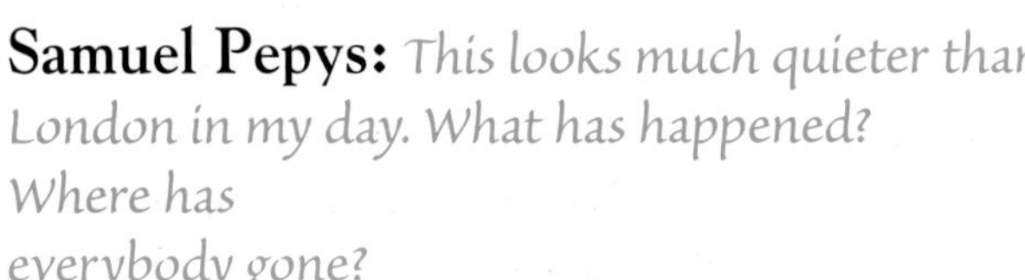

Samuel Pepys: *This looks much quieter than London in my day. What has happened? Where has everybody gone?*

Flora Thompson:
You've only seen the country so far! If you want to know how fast life is changing, you'll have to visit the cities – if you're brave enough! Why don't I take you to London – by train?

Sir Geoffrey Luttrell : *A train…?*

Samuel Pepys: *What's a train?*

A RAILWAY STATION

Flora Thompson: *Here we are – London! What do you think of our trains?*

Sir Geoffrey Luttrell: *Frightening! Much faster than horses but the people don't seem worried by the speed.*

Flora Thompson: *They did when trains first appeared 60 years ago. People expected to die if the train went any faster than a horse. They also thought that trains would kill the animals they passed in the fields. Now people travel all over the country by train to find new jobs or to go on holiday, and the trains bring fresh food into the towns – butter, milk, fruit and vegetables. Before trains many people in towns couldn't get fresh food.*

ENTERTAINMENT

Sir Geoffrey Luttrell: *Doesn't anyone stay at home any more?*

Flora Thompson: *Oh yes! We don't leave home all that often, even though we can go much further now. We have lots of things to do to entertain ourselves in the village: there's nothing like a good old sing-song round the piano with all your friends. If you want to go out for a sing-song you could go to the music halls. Lots of people like those shows but I prefer to see plays at the theatre.*

Samuel Pepys: *Is that where we are going now? I know lots of plays!*

Flora Thompson: *No. We're going to see something new! It's a cricket match, England against Australia. That's W.G. Grace, England's captain. He's the best cricketer in the world.*

Samuel Pepys: *Why aren't all these people at work?*

Flora Thompson: *Many people get Saturday afternoon off. In winter thousands of them go to watch Football League or Cup matches. Watching sport is very popular now that people can travel by train to follow their teams. There couldn't be leagues or professional sports games before the railways came. Mind you, some of the crowds at the football get into fights if their team loses!*

Sir Geoffrey Luttrell: *It doesn't look very interesting. I think a joust or bear-baiting would get a bigger crowd. Where else can we go?*

Flora Thompson: *We could go to the seaside; we could see if my cousin would like to come. Let's see if she's at work.*

A FACTORY

Flora Thompson: *This is the factory where my cousin works. They make matches. People use them to light fires.*

Sir Geoffrey Luttrell: *Don't* these *women have time off work on a Saturday?*

Flora Thompson: *These girls don't. They have to work ten hours every day. My cousin says that many of them fall ill from the chemicals used to make the matches. If they complain they lose part of their wages. Two years ago the girls went on strike because they were being treated so badly. They stayed on strike for three weeks and in the end the employers gave in and improved their conditions but they're still not very good.*

Samuel Pepys: *Why don't they work somewhere else?*

Flora Thompson: *There aren't many jobs. Most people in towns work in large factories. A hundred years ago most people still worked on farms but it's changed a lot since then. Now over half the population live in towns and work in factories and offices.*

They do get holidays. Some of them get a week and some get two weeks – that's when they take the train to the seaside.

Sir Geoffrey Luttrell: *Is your cousin here?*

Flora Thompson: *I don't know, I'll ask someone where she is.*

...My cousin's husband's been hurt at work. She's gone to find him at the docks.

Samuel Pepys: *Let's go and see her there, if it's not too far.*

THE DOCKS

Sir Geoffrey Luttrell: *What happens here?*

Samuel Pepys: *I know the answer to that. These are the docks where ships arrive from America and Africa.*

Flora Thompson: *And from much further away than that.*

Plenty of ships come from Australia and New Zealand these days. Some of them are refrigerated. That means that they can bring frozen meat from the other side of the world for us to eat.

Sir Geoffrey Luttrell: *Don't you grow enough food for your people then?*

Flora Thompson: *Not any more. There are 40 million people in the country now.*

The harvest is still important to us but we import food from all over the world. People no longer starve because of one bad harvest.

Samuel Pepys: *These men look as if they could do with more food.*

Flora Thompson: *They're the dockers who load and unload the ships. They turn up every day hoping for work. Some days they end up fighting each other if there's not enough work for them all. My cousin says that men can get seriously hurt. That could be what happened to her husband. But things are improving since they formed a union and went on strike last year. Now they get an extra penny an hour for their work.*

Now, I must look for my cousin …

… She's gone to the hospital with her husband. We'll try there next.

A HOSPITAL

Samuel Pepys: *Is he badly hurt?*

Flora Thompson: *His leg was crushed by a box that fell off a crane. He's going to need an operation on his leg.*

Samuel Pepys: *That will hurt. Have I ever told you about* my *operation?*

Sir Geoffrey Luttrell: *Many times, Sam, many times.*

Flora Thompson: *It won't hurt. They'll use an anaesthetic so he won't feel anything and they'll use antiseptics in the ward to kill any germs that are around. He's got a good chance of getting better. I'm glad I wasn't around a hundred years ago and needed an operation; it's all a lot safer these days, but it will cost my cousin's family a lot of money. The treatment isn't free.*

Sir Geoffrey Luttrell: *What's that woman doing over there? Is she a nun?*

Flora Thompson: *She's one of the new women doctors. The men don't like having women doctors but there's a few of them now and they're very good.*

Samuel Pepys: *Women doctors! Who would have imagined that? What else do women do these days?*

Flora Thompson: *I'll show you. We'll walk across the park and then you'll get a surprise!*

Sir Geoffrey Luttrell: *Is your cousin remaining here with her husband?*

Flora Thompson: *No. She must go back to work. They need all she can earn.*

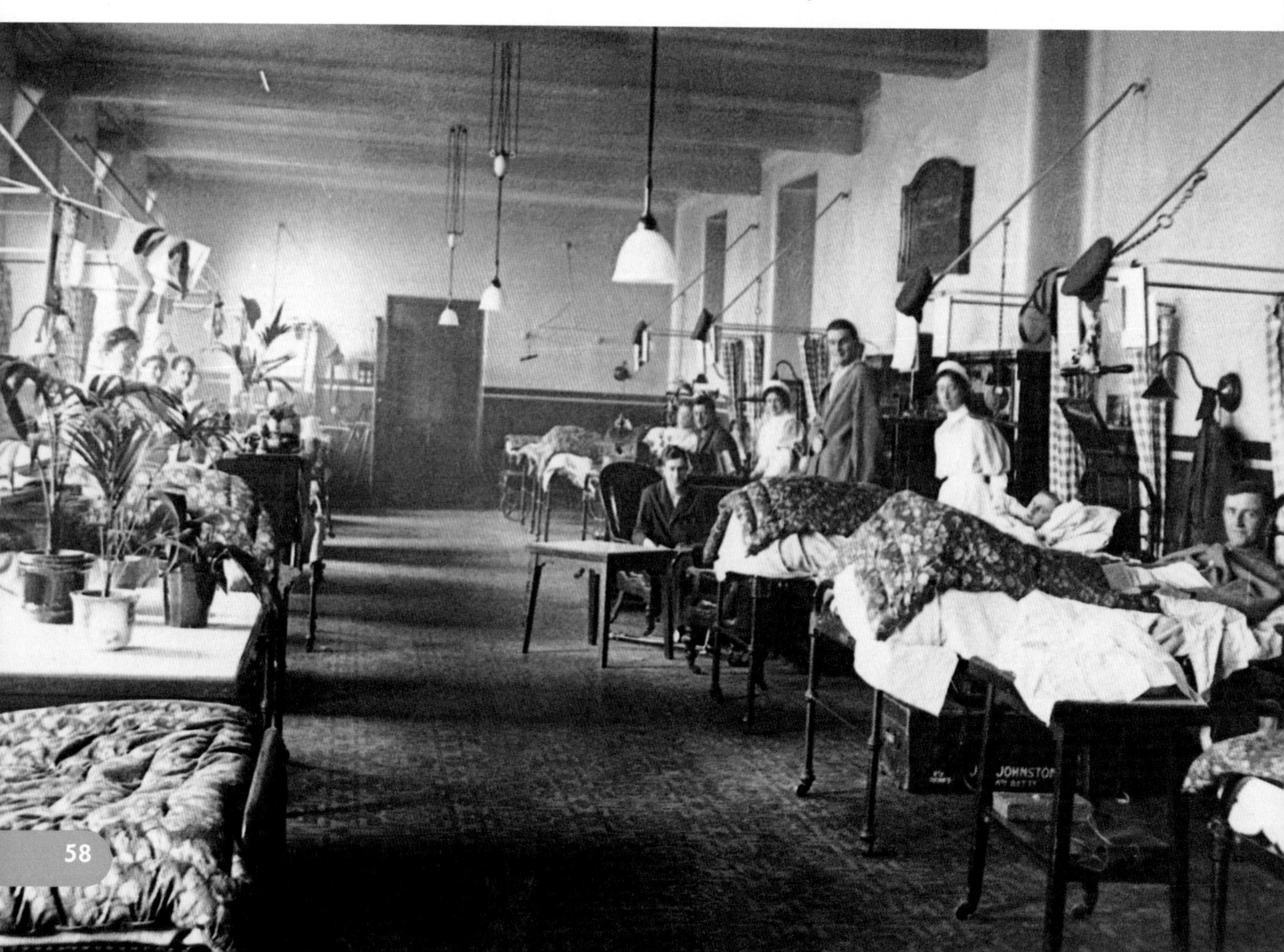

THE POLICE

Sir Geoffrey Luttrell: *Who owns this land? Why doesn't he grow food here?*

Flora Thompson: *It doesn't belong to one man. It belongs to all of us. It's a public park. The people in the city have the chance to get fresh air, play games and listen to bands. They can get away from all the smoke in their homes and the factories.*

Samuel Pepys: *Who's that?*

Flora Thompson: *He's a policeman. He's chasing that pickpocket. He'll get him soon.*

Samuel Pepys: *It'll be a public hanging. I expect there'll be a good crowd.*

Flora Thompson: *Oh, we don't have public executions any more, and only murderers get hanged these days. That thief might be sent to prison to do hard labour.*

The police are really busy in the towns and cities. At home we read about all the murders and robberies in the newspapers but it's not like that in the country. In Candleford our policeman sometimes stops a cyclist for speeding, and he tries to catch poachers, but he spends most of his time working in his garden!

Samuel Pepys: *Who's the statue of?*

Flora Thompson: *That's Robert Peel, he started the first police force ...*

THE QUEEN

Flora Thompson: *Here's your surprise – Queen Victoria. We have a woman ruling the country. God bless Queen Victoria!*

Samuel Pepys: *Everyone seems to love your Queen.*

Flora Thompson: *We do now. Until about ten years ago, Victoria wasn't popular at all. After her husband Prince Albert died, she shut herself away and never came out in public. A lot of people wanted to get rid of the monarchy completely. Then the Queen started travelling round the country again, and everyone loved her Golden Jubilee three years ago. There were parties in every village and town. We had one in Lark Rise with sports, roundabouts and tightrope walkers. It was a wonderful day, the greatest I've ever known.*

Sir Geoffrey Luttrell: *So does your Queen make all the important decisions about how the country is run, like the kings in my time?*

Flora Thompson: *No, the Queen doesn't do that. That's the job of the Prime Minister and the other politicians. They really govern the country. They're the people you ought to see.*

THE PRIME MINISTER

Flora Thompson: *That's Mr Gladstone. He's been Prime Minister three times already and he's hoping to win the next election too.*

Samuel Pepys: *Why is he talking to these common people? Most of them are too poor to have a vote in elections.*

Flora Thompson: *No, these days nearly all men can vote in elections to choose their MPs. Mr Gladstone wants to win their votes – and he will too. He often makes speeches that last four hours, and he travels all over the country by train to make speeches to the people. You wouldn't believe he's 81. People call him 'The Grand Old Man'.*

Samuel Pepys: *So the Levellers got their way at last. They were people in my time who wanted every man to have the vote. Can women vote too?*

Flora Thompson: *No, but men can't stop us having the vote for ever. Women are better educated now and some are even going to university, like those doctors we saw. Lots of women are campaigning to win the vote. We'll be able to vote soon!*

Samuel Pepys: *Never!*

IMPROVEMENTS

Samuel Pepys: *What have these politicians done to improve people's lives?*

Flora Thompson: *A lot has changed since ordinary men got the vote. Better houses are being built. Food is better: shopkeepers can't put chalk into bread or find other ways of cheating customers. I think the most important change is that clean water is piped into towns and different pipes take away sewage. That makes the towns a lot healthier. Since Louis Pasteur discovered that germs cause disease we have been trying to stop germs and diseases from spreading. Everybody has to be vaccinated against smallpox and other diseases. On average people are living longer than ever before – until they're over 50.*

Sir Geoffrey Luttrell: *What I like best are these street lights.*

Flora Thompson: *You should go inside houses. Some of them have electric lighting and the lights come on at the flick of a switch – it's even better than gas.*

Samuel Pepys: *There's one thing that hasn't changed – all the horses in the streets. You'll always need horses!*

Could you live in 1890?

It's time for your next important decision. This page helps you to decide whether you would like to live in 1890.

Activity A

Would you like to live in the country or the city in 1890?

If you have to stay in 1890 you can choose to live in either the countryside or the city. Write an essay explaining your choice. You could use these sentence starters to help you to plan your paragraphs.

I would/would not like to live in the countryside.
One reason for this is that . . .
Another reason is . . .
I would/would not like to live in the city.
One reason for this is that . . .
Another reason is . . .
I would therefore prefer to live in the countryside/ the city. The most important reason is . . .

Activity B

1 a) Draw your own copy of the chart below. Fill in the columns with reasons to support each statement. Include things you would miss about life today as well as things, good or bad, about 1890.

I would prefer to live in 1890 rather than today because . . .	I would not really want to live in 1890 but I could put up with it because . . .	I would hate to live in 1890 because . . .

b) Put a star against the three reasons that are most important in helping you to decide whether you want to live in 1890. They can all be in one column or from different columns.

2 Draw your own copy of the pendulum on page 4. Draw the arrow on your pendulum to show your decision about whether you would like to live in 1890.

3 Explain your decision. You could write paragraphs giving the reasons for living in 1890, the reasons against living in 1890, and explaining which reason was most important in reaching your decision, and why. You can get a sheet from your teacher to help you.

Activity C

It's time to leave 1890 – but have you got everything you need to get home? Have you found anyone who can help you to mend your computer? If you haven't, you have two choices:

a) stay in one of the three periods you have visited. If you choose this option then turn to page 66

b) travel forward into the twentieth century in the hope that you can find a computer expert to help you. If you choose this option turn to page 64.

1.5 ORAL HISTORY – INVESTIGATING THE TWENTIETH CENTURY

So you've decided to look for a computer expert in the 1900s? Well, you won't have to go searching through lots of books to find one. All you have to do is some **oral history** research! Oral history is what people say about the past, about the things they remember from when they were younger. This is a very interesting way of getting evidence about what life was like for your parents, grandparents, friends and relatives when they were your age.

Their answers may surprise you. Life has changed very quickly in the last hundred years. In the 1900s it changed far more quickly than in any other century. Your grandparents had very different childhoods from you. Even your parents' childhoods were quite different because things have been changing so rapidly.

On the opposite page you will see a questionnaire which you can use to collect oral evidence. You can put the questions to one of your grandparents or someone else over 50 years old. You might like to record the answers on tape, especially the answers to the questions from number 4 onwards, as this will be easier than writing them down. You could play recordings of interesting memories to the rest of your class and build up a class 'Oral history' library. You can use the sorting grid on page 5 of this book to suggest topics that your interviewee could talk about in questions 4–8.

ACTIVITY

You still need an expert to mend the computer in your time capsule, so here's just one last question: in which decade were computers first used in lessons in schools?

If you get the right answer you'll be able to land your time capsule in the right decade, find an expert to help you to mend your computer, and then go home!

Life in the 1900s

Researcher: ______________________ Interviewee: ______________________

1 Were you at school in the 1930s 1940s 1950s 1960s ?

2 Where did you grow up? ______________________

3 Which of these did you have in your house as a child?

TELEPHONE TV COMPUTER RADIO FRIDGE WASHING MACHINE

4 Has life become more comfortable since you were a child? YES/NO

How? ______________________

____

____

5 Have school and work changed since you were a child? YES/NO

How? ______________________

____

____

6 Have holidays and leisure changed? YES/NO

How? ______________________

____

____

7 Are people healthier today? YES/NO

How? ______________________

____

____

8 Are people more equal today? YES/NO

How? ______________________

____

____

9 Do you think that life has changed

SLOWLY / STEADILY / QUICKLY / VERY QUICKLY since you were a child?

10 What do you think have been **a)** the best **b)** the worst changes?

a) ______________________

b) ______________________

1.6 CHANGES AND CONTINUITIES FROM 1000 TO 2000

◆ Timeline 1: comfort

This timeline shows you the main changes and continuities (things that stay the same) across the centuries. It covers the first topic in your sorting grid: comfort. The other four topics are on the next eight pages. You have probably worked out a lot of this for yourself on your travels through time but the timelines give you a quick summary – and the questions will make sure that you understand the main points!

ACTIVITY

1 List two things on the timeline that were continuities for hundreds of years.

2 a) Decide which was the most important change.

b) Explain your choice. It's up to you to explain why this change was the most important. It could be that the change affected the most people; or the effects lasted for the longest time; or it seemed the most dramatic change at the time.

	1200	1300	1400–1500
TOILETS	Garderobes for the rich. The poor dug pits or went in the forest		
HEATING AND LIGHTING	Fire Candles		
UTENSILS	Pottery Metal knives and spoons Pewter for wealthy people	Forks	
TRANSPORT	Horses and donkeys with carts		
FOOD	Water, ale, soup, vegetables, fish and brown bread for poor The rich also ate white bread and meat		Better, more varied diet. Meat for ordinary people
CLOTHING	Simple, undyed clothing for poor The rich wore colourful, more ornate clothes		More varied and better quality clothing
HOMES	One-storey houses		Warmer, better built houses; more use of glass and stone

1200 1300 1400 1500

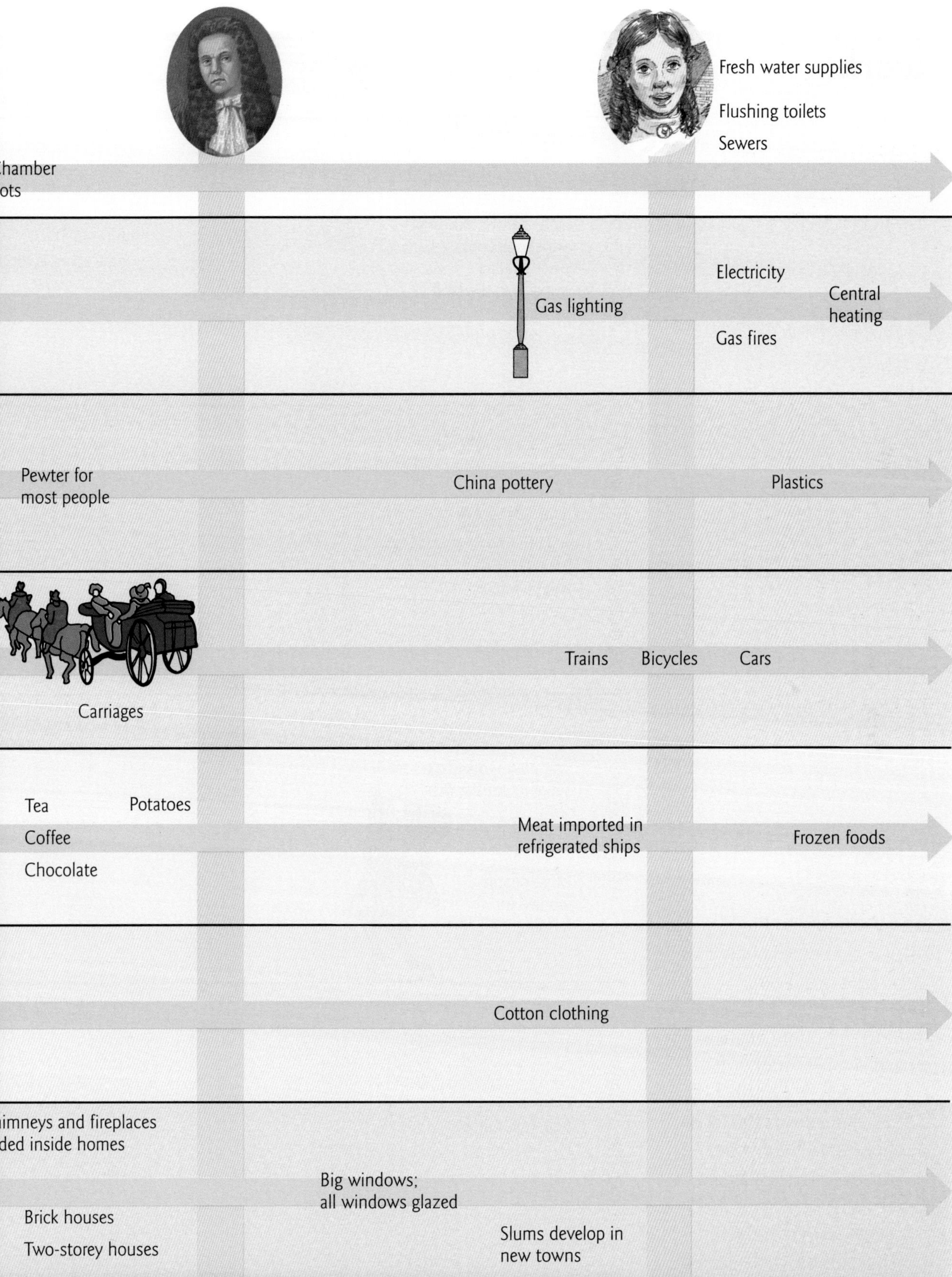
Chamber pots
Fresh water supplies
Flushing toilets
Sewers
Gas lighting
Electricity
Gas fires
Central heating
Pewter for most people
China pottery
Plastics
Carriages
Trains
Bicycles
Cars
Tea
Coffee
Chocolate
Potatoes
Meat imported in refrigerated ships
Frozen foods
Cotton clothing
himneys and fireplaces
dded inside homes
Brick houses
Two-storey houses
Big windows;
all windows glazed
Slums develop in new towns
1600
1700
1800
1900
2000

Timeline 2: work

EDUCATION	Only a small minority went to school. Most children worked on the land	Introduction of ma new schools for th middle classes
DEVELOPMENTS IN INDUSTRY	Local industries, e.g. coal mining, ironworking, the cloth trade, shipbuilding	
TYPES OF WORK	The poor worked as servants for the rich Most people worked in farming	
COUNTRY VS TOWN	Only 10% of population lived in towns	
	1200 · 1300 · 1400 · 1500	

ACTIVITY

1 List two things on the timeline that were continuities for hundreds of years.

2 a) Decide which was the most important change.

b) Explain your choice. It's up to you to explain why this change was the most important. It could be that the change affected the most people; or the effects lasted for the longest time; or it seemed the most dramatic change at the time.

School is compulsory up to age:

11	14	15	16

Developments of factories and steam engines

Laws to improve working hours and conditions

Machinery introduced on some farms

Huge increases in number of domestic servants

Many people working in factories and industry, e.g. coal and iron, pottery, shipbuilding, chemicals

New jobs in communications, entertainment and computing

Towns growing steadily

50% of population living in towns

1600 1700 1800 1900 2000

Timeline 3: enjoyment

	1200	1300	1400	1500
HOLIDAYS	Church holy days			
	Pilgrimages			
HOME ENTERTAINMENT	Singing			
	Dancing			Printed boc[ks] for reading
	Storytelling			
GOING OUT	Church festivals and saints' days			
	Fairs, jesters, travelling actors			
SPECTATOR SPORTS	Bear baiting			
	Cock fighting			
SPORTS TO PLAY	Football			Footba[ll]
	Hunting			
	Archery			

ACTIVITY

1 List two things on the timeline that were continuities for hundreds of years.

2 **a)** Decide which was the most important change.

b) Explain your choice. It's up to you to explain why this change was the most important. It could be that the change affected the most people; or the effects lasted for the longest time; or it seemed the most dramatic change at the time.

Bank Holiday Act, 1871

The rich travel to historic sites

The rich travel overseas

Railway tours

Seaside holidays

First Butlins holiday camp opened, 1936

Bus tours/ car travel

Overseas package holidays

Singing and playing piano or other musical instruments

Radio

TV

Computers

Theatres

Libraries

Music halls

Museums

Cinemas

Horse racing

Boxing

Watching professional sport, e.g. football and cricket

Football

Football

Golf

Cricket

Tennis

Badminton

Athletics

Cycling

Basketball

Volleyball

Baseball

Snowboarding

1600 | 1700 | 1800 | 1900 | 2000

Timeline 4: danger

CRIME AND PUNISHMENT

Hue and cry

Village constables introduced

Thieves and murderers hanged

MEDICINE

Herbal cures

Bleeding

DISEASE

1348 Black Death

AVERAGE LIFE EXPECTANCY

40

40

1200 1300 1400 1500

ACTIVITY

1 List two things on the timeline that were continuities for hundreds of years.

2 **a)** Decide which was the most important change.

b) Explain your choice. It's up to you to explain why this change was the most important. It could be that the change affected the most people; or the effects lasted for the longest time; or it seemed the most dramatic change at the time.

Town watchmen

Police service formed

Thieves sent to prison

Prisons reformed

Witches burned

End of public hangings

End of executions

National Health Service – free medical treatment for all

Vaccinations for smallpox

Possible vaccinations for cancer

Cleaner hospitals

X-rays

Pepys is lucky to survive a gallstone operation

Dirty hospitals

Anaesthetics

Antiseptics

Blood transfusions

Transplant surgery

Plague!

1665 plague in London

Rapid growth of towns increased spread of infectious diseases

Germs discovered to be the cause of infectious disease. Rapid improvements in provision of public services, e.g. running water, sewers

45

45

50

75

1600 1700 1800 1900 2000

Timeline 5: equality

	1200	1300	1400	1500
RACE				
RELIGION	Jews expelled from Britain			Anyone who not attend Church of En services was punished by or imprisonm
FREEDOM	40% of people were villeins – **unfree**	1348 Black Death + 1381 Peasants' Revolt (REVOLT)	help lead to	freedom for everybody
STATUS OF WOMEN	Many marriages arranged by parents			
VOTING				

ACTIVITY

1. List two things on the timeline that were continuities for hundreds of years.
2. **a)** Decide which was the most important change.
   b) Explain your choice. It's up to you to explain why this change was the most important. It could be that the change affected the most people; or the effects lasted for the longest time; or it seemed the most dramatic change at the time.
3. Now look at all the timelines together.
   a) When did change begin to speed up?
   b) When did change happen fastest?

Slave trading from Africa to the Americas

Slow increase in the black population of Britain

Abolition of slavery, 1833

Troops from the colonies fought in both World Wars

Windrush immigration from the colonies to fill job vacancies in the 1950s

Only members of Church of England were allowed to vote or become MPs

Members of other religions allowed to vote

Jews allowed to return to Britain

Introduction of laws to protect equal rights

Women able to own property and attend university

First women MPs

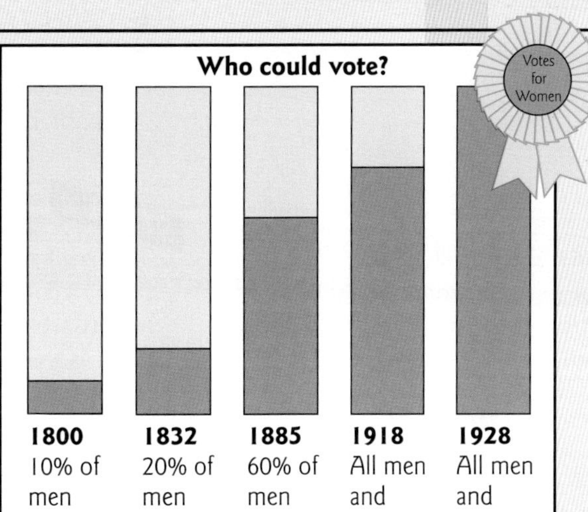

All people aged over 18

1600 1700 1800 1900 2000

1.7 HISTORY TREK!

Pull everything together in an essay to explain when you would most like to have lived

ACTIVITY

You have visited three periods: 1330, 1669 and 1890. Use the work you have already done and the timelines on pages 66–75 to help you to write a short essay explaining which period you would choose to live in if you could not live today.

Writing an essay is like going on a journey. You need to plan carefully and to know where you are going (what your conclusion is) before you start. The framework of the essay is shown as a journey into space – a History Trek – on pages 78–79. It has seven stages and you will be pleased to know that you already have notes for most of them!

The Trek and the advice below will help you to write your essay. Remember: the argument of your essay must be easy to follow. That means that you have to help your reader to understand clearly which period of time you have chosen to live in – and why.

Good luck!

I would prefer to live here rather than in the 21st century.
I do not really want to live here but I could put up with it if I had to.
I would hate to live here.

STAGE 1

Pre-flight check

Check the clipboard on page 78. Make sure all your answers are 'Yes!' If not, you won't even take off!

STAGE 2

Countdown – the introduction

The introduction is the most important and tricky part of the flight. It is surprisingly difficult. Think carefully about what you are going to write before the countdown begins.

Key tips:

- Make it interesting and lively so the reader wants to read on.
- Keep it short but make sure the reader knows which time you have chosen to live in.
- Say which criteria were most important in making your choice (look back to page 5).

STAGE 3

Blast off – your least favourite

This is where you explain which time period you would least like to live in. Don't just give the date; give two or three reasons why you would not want to live then.

Key tips:

- Think of this as a hamburger paragraph.
- Look back to the pendulum and the activity for the time you have chosen not to live in (either page 25, 43 or 63) for some ideas.

STAGE 4

Into orbit – your second favourite

This is a little more complicated. Think of this as a double hamburger. You need to give reasons why you might like to live in this time, as well as reasons why you would not.

Key tips:

- Begin by saying which period of time is your second choice.
- Then give a reason or reasons why you might like to live then.
- Give reasons why you would not want to live then. Make sure these are more important than the reasons why you might have chosen this time.

Space walk – your first choice

This is just like Stage 4. It's another double hamburger but in reverse!

Key tips:

- Begin by saying which period you have chosen to live in.
- Give one or two reasons why you might have decided against living then.
- Give the reasons why you decided to choose that time. Make sure these are more important than the reasons against this period.

Touchdown – the conclusion

Key tips:

- Keep your conclusion brief. State the period you have chosen.
- Explain why living in your chosen period would be better or worse than living today. What would you miss about today? What was better in the past?

Press check

Do not miss out Stage 7. By this stage in the Trek you have put a good deal of hard work into your essay. Do not spoil everything by handing in a piece of work which has lots of mistakes in it. Check your essay carefully. Improve parts that you are not happy with.

In-flight menu

Here are some phrases and sentence starters that you could use in your essay – to begin paragraphs or link to the next topic.

The time period I have chosen is . . .

If I have to live in the past I would live in . . .

I have decided that I would/would not like to live in ______ because . . .

What I liked/disliked most about ______ was . . .

The most important reason for choosing/not choosing ______ was . . .

Although there are both things that I like and things that I dislike about living in ______ I have decided . . .

Although I could live in ______ I would prefer to live in . . .

What I would miss most about life today is . . .

Although I would like ______ in ______ there are more things I dislike about living then.

Ten top tips for revising and editing

Creative suggestions:

1. Have you actually answered the question?
2. Is there anything missing? Have you supported all your arguments with evidence?
3. Is there anything that isn't clear or accurate?
4. Do you think the writing is interesting/enjoyable to read?
5. Is your work neatly presented? Do you want to add a front cover or illustrate your work?

Technical suggestions:

6. Use a dictionary to check the spelling of any words that you are not sure of.
7. Full stops must be used at the end of every sentence. Have you used full stops regularly?
8. Check that you have used capital letters to start names, as well as every new sentence.
9. Check that you have written in paragraphs. Have you left an indent (started your writing 2.5 cm from the margin) at the beginning of each new paragraph?
10. Check the length of your sentences. Put in some short, sharp sentences. It adds variety and interest.

THE HISTORY TREK

STAGE 1: PRE-FLIGHT CHECK

1 Are you clear on the question?
2 Have you completed your research?
3 Are you sure of your argument?
4 Do you have enough evidence to support this argument?

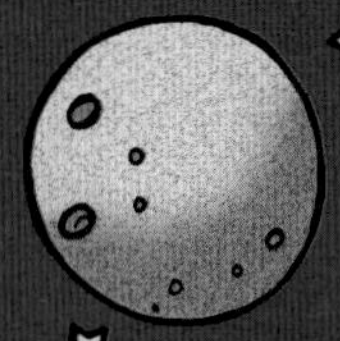

This is the part I hate the most!

I hope we get a good start...

STAGE 2: COUNTDOWN – THE INTRODUCTION

- Give a brief answer to the question.
- Make your reader want to read on.

STAGE 3: BLAST OFF – YOUR LEAST FAVOURITE

- Say which time period you would least like to live in.
- Explain the reasons why you do not want to live then.

STAGE 4: INTO ORBIT – YOUR SECOND FAVOURITE

- Say which time period is your second choice.
- Give a reason or two why you could live then.
- Give the reasons why you decided not to live then.

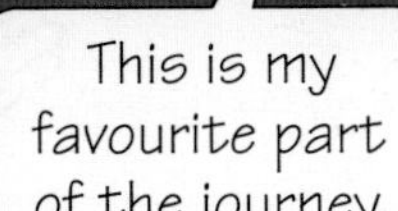

This is my favourite part of the journey.

STAGE 5: SPACE WALK – YOUR FIRST CHOICE

- Say which time period you have chosen to live in.
- Give a reason or two why it might be difficult to live then.
- Give the reasons why you have chosen to live then.

STAGE 6: TOUCHDOWN – THE CONCLUSION

- Explain whether the period you have chosen would be better or worse than living today.

STAGE 7: PRESS CHECK

- Check your work carefully. Use the ten top tips on page 77 to check and improve your essay.

Home at last!

25 Oct. 2015
TV NEWS
Tonight's fast-breaking news is good news! The time capsule containing a class of school children from Newtown High School has returned home safely. On board are all thirty children, although there is no sign of their history teacher, Mr Mullins. They were returning from a school trip to Ancient Rome when there was a computer failure. They seem to have had many adventures on their way home, but in the end were able to find help in fixing their computer. We hope to have interviews with the children in our next bulletin.
Am I glad to be home!
How will we explain about Mr Mullins?
Never mind him, how will we explain about Sir Geoffrey, Flora and Sam?
We can take them home next time we go on a time trip.
Next time - you must be joking!

SECTION 2

WHY WERE THEIR LIVES SO DIFFERENT?

Explaining the big changes

In Section 1 you met us, real people from the past, and you discovered a lot about our lives.

Section 2 helps you to investigate WHY those important changes happened. You are going to investigate three of the most important turning-points in British history.

In some ways our lives were similar but there were also very important differences. Important changes happened between Sir Geoffrey's lifetime and mine and between my lifetime and Flora's.

Freedom

In 1300 many people – the villeins – were not free to live and work where they wanted. By 1500 everyone was free.
WHY?

Religion

In the Middle Ages everyone was Catholic and no other religions were tolerated. Now people have different religions and we no longer burn people to death because of their beliefs.
WHY?

Towns

In the Middle Ages nearly everyone lived and worked in the country. Now nearly everyone lives in towns.
WHY?

2.1 WHY DID THE VILLEINS WIN THEIR FREEDOM?

◆ *The Black Death*

... The rat scuttled off the ship. It stopped, sniffed the air for the smell of food – and scratched. It scratched because it was carrying fleas. Together the rat and fleas were about to kill two million people in Britain. The fleas were carrying bubonic plague, the **Black Death**!

That ship arrived on the south coast of England in 1348. Soon people in nearby towns and villages fell ill. They felt cold and tired. Black swellings called buboes grew in their armpits and groins. Then they felt hot and feverish and the headaches began, worse than any they had ever known. They became unconscious – and then they died.

At least 40 per cent of the population died within a year. Imagine the Luttrell village of Gerneham. About 300 people lived there before the plague arrived. Just a few weeks later there were fewer than 200 shocked survivors. Whole families died. Husbands and wives lost partners and children. Children lost their parents.

What has the Black Death got to do with the villeins winning their freedom? Think back to Gerneham in Sir Geoffrey's time (see page 6). It was difficult to feed all the people. The freemen's wages were low. Some villeins, like Piers, wanted to be free but they also knew that if there was a bad harvest then the poor freemen and their families would starve.

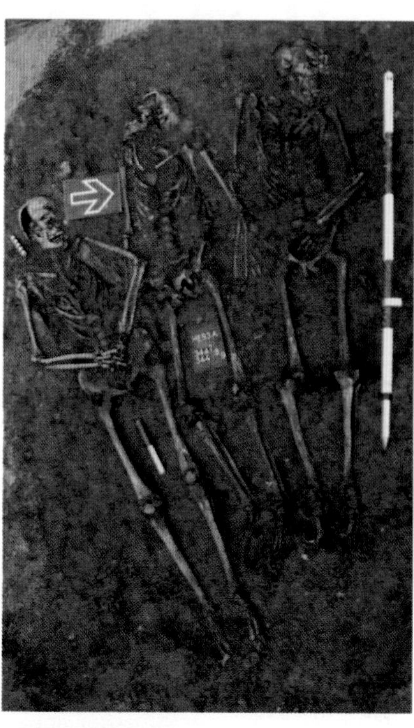

SOURCE 1 The Black Death killed so many, so quickly, that the dead could not be buried in individual graves. Large pits were dug and the bodies were piled in together. Archaeologists can learn a lot from the skeletons about the height, teeth and general health of people in the 1300s.

ACTIVITY

On your own:

1 Read the top half of page 83 about landowners, freemen and villeins 'Before the Black Death'.

2 Before the Black Death there were plenty of workers. Which group of people was in the best position then? Explain your choice.

3 Who struggled the most before the Black Death? Explain your choice.

4 How did the Black Death change:

a) the population

b) the wages of freemen

c) the price of food?

Now divide into groups of two or three.

Your teacher will tell you whether your group are landowners, freemen or villeins.

5 Read your box at the bottom of page 83, 'After the Black Death'.

6 Discuss which choice, A or B, you are going to make.

7 Explain why you made that choice and not the other one.

BEFORE THE BLACK DEATH (Population about 6 million)

The landowner – Sir Andrew Luttrell (he inherited the estate when his father died)

I give the villeins land to grow their food. In return they work on my land. I also pay freemen to do extra work. I get high prices for the food grown on my land.

People need the work so I only pay low wages. It's so easy to get workers; perhaps I should free some villeins. Then I'll get their land back and make more money from growing food there.

The freeman – Richard's son

I own some land. I grow my food on it and get extra money by working for Sir Andrew when he needs me.

Sir Andrew pays me low wages because he can easily find other workers. I need to work hard on my own land to feed my family. If I need extra food it is very expensive.

The villein – Piers's son

I work on Sir Andrew's land two days a week. In return he has given me a little land to grow food for my family.

Sir Andrew says he may give me my freedom. My dad always wanted to be free, but where will I find work? I wouldn't have any land to grow food on then either.

AFTER THE BLACK DEATH (Population about 3 million)

Many villeins are dead. I need more workers or I will have nothing to eat or sell. I have two choices:

A Free the rest of the villeins then pay the workers more so that they want to work for me. *Or*

B Ask the King to make a new law saying that:
- no villeins can be freed
- freemen must be paid the same wages as before the plague.

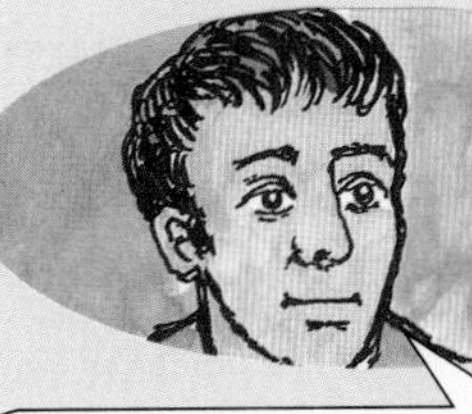

There are fewer workers so Sir Andrew needs me. This might be my big chance. I have two choices:

A Stay in the village and earn the same wages as before. It may not be exciting but at least I'm alive after the plague. *Or*

B Demand higher wages and tell Sir Andrew that if he doesn't give me more money then I'll leave the village. Another landowner is bound to pay me more.

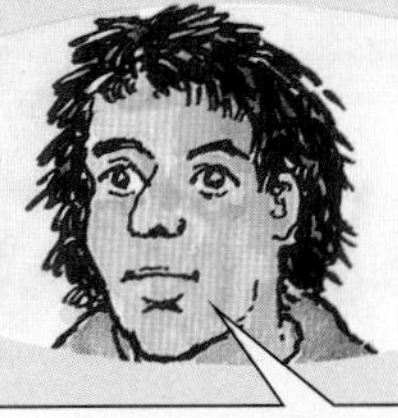

Sir Andrew needs workers. Freemen expect higher pay but I don't get paid for my work. I have two choices:

A Demand my freedom so I can earn more money. I'll promise to work for him so long as he gives me a good wage. *Or*

B Stay as a villein. It's what my family has always done, and at least I know I'll keep my strips of land.

ACTIVITY A

1 Divide into two groups – freemen and villeins.
2 Read the information on Stage 1: 1350–1370s.
3 Decide how angry you are about the way you are being treated by the landowners. Which level are you at on the Anger Index below?
4 Explain why you chose that level on the Anger Index.
If you are at level 5 of the Anger Index then you are so angry that you are ready to rebel against the King and the landowners. You will have to fight, so you will need:
- everyone in your group to join in, *and*
- the help of the other group – the villeins or freemen – who must also have reached at least level 4.

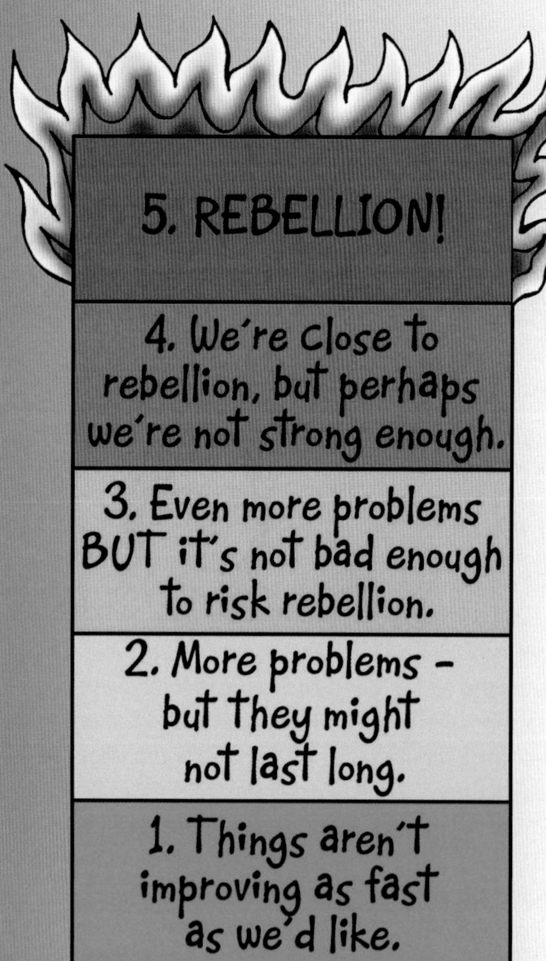

5. REBELLION!
4. We're close to rebellion, but perhaps we're not strong enough.
3. Even more problems BUT it's not bad enough to risk rebellion.
2. More problems – but they might not last long.
1. Things aren't improving as fast as we'd like.

◆ What happened next?

Stage 1: 1350–1370s

The landowners like Sir Andrew chose option B, so it did not matter what choice the freemen and villeins made! The King made a law called the STATUTE OF LABOURERS. This said that:

1 Villeins were not allowed to become free.
2 Freemen had to work for the same wages as before the Black Death.

It was difficult to protest. Freemen and villeins did have weapons, because the King said that they must have weapons in case there was a war, but the landowners were trained knights with well-equipped soldiers.

How did the freemen react?

The freemen did not like the new law. It seemed to rule out their big chance of getting higher wages and improving their lives. However, the law couldn't put the clock back. Slowly and steadily the freemen did begin to earn higher wages. This happened because landowners were desperately short of workers. They did not want their workers leaving to find higher wages somewhere else so each year they paid them a little more.

As a result, the freemen gradually became better off. They were able to improve their lives, but more slowly than they wanted.

How did the villeins react?

The villeins hated the new law. They had thought they had a chance of freedom but the landowners would not grant villeins their freedom. If a villein ran away he was chased, brought back and punished in the local court. If the landowner did not catch him, he could punish the man's relatives instead.

In many villages people began to complain, but there were never enough people involved to build up a major protest.

Stage 2: 1377 – war!

King Edward III was a great soldier. In 1346 and 1356 he won great victories over France at the battles of Crécy and Poitiers. English and Welsh archers slaughtered the French knights before they could get near to the English army. However, Edward III died in 1377. The new King was his nine-year-old grandson, Richard II.

The French began to fight back. In 1377 they attacked many English towns. They burned several coastal towns. A hundred local men were killed defending Rottingdean in Sussex. Next, the French army landed on the Isle of Wight where they looted and burned houses.

As a result of these attacks the government decided to collect a tax. The money would be spent on paying for more soldiers to defend the English coast against the French. In those days people did not pay taxes every year. In fact they had paid no taxes for twelve years between 1359 and 1371. When they did pay tax, people paid different amounts, depending upon how rich or poor they were. But this time, in 1377, the government introduced a new tax called a POLL TAX. Everyone paid the same amount, four pence – a whole day's pay for a skilled worker.

Stage 3: 1380 – tax, tax, tax!

The French attacks continued. In 1378 they burned towns all along the coast of Cornwall and made the people pay them large amounts of money to leave them alone. Next, Sussex and Kent were attacked again. People began to complain that the lords and knights were not doing enough to defend them against the French. They complained even more when they had to pay another Poll Tax in 1379 and again in 1380. This time everyone had to pay twelve pence a head, three times higher than the 1377 tax. They also began to think about what they might do when the tax collectors arrived, yet again, in their villages. Should they just pay, or try to hide from the tax collectors, or even rebel?

	1377	1380
Bocking	318	216
Felsted	263	165
Sturmer	150	113
Stebbing	252	155
Halstead	381	242
All Essex	**47,962**	**30,533**

SOURCE 2 Documents still exist that tell us how many people paid the Poll Taxes of 1377 and 1380. Here are the totals in some Essex villages and for the whole county.

ACTIVITY B

1 Read about Stage 2 in your groups.
  a) Which level of the Anger Index have you now reached?
  b) Explain why you chose that level.

2 Read Stage 3 in your groups.
  a) Which level of the Anger Index have you reached by 1380?
  b) Explain why you are or are not ready to rebel.

Stage 4: 1381 – the tax collectors return!

Many people hated the Poll Tax of 1380. It was a much higher tax than they had paid before and it didn't seem fair that everyone, from dukes to villeins, paid the same amount. When the tax collectors came round again, early in 1381, many people hid from them. In total, there were nearly half a million fewer people in the tax lists in 1381 than in 1377. Although people were angry about the Poll Tax, they decided to avoid paying instead of taking the risk of protesting and rebelling.

Then came shocking news. The government was angry too. It was sending out new tax collectors to find all those missing taxpayers and force them to pay up. Perhaps they would have to pay more as a punishment. Now many people felt that they had only one choice left – a big protest against the tax and the way the country was being governed.

Now we'll *have* to pay this new Poll Tax. The collectors will find us this time.
It's a waste of our money. We keep paying but the government hasn't stopped the French from attacking us.
The only thing the government does is to stop us getting our freedom.
And earning higher wages.

The rebellion began in Kent and Essex. Tax collectors were attacked. Tax records were destroyed. Villagers gathered together and planned their protest. Many of them were better-off villagers who were used to organising men for work and defences against invaders. Their leader was Wat Tyler. They rode and marched towards London, determined to tell the young king, Richard II, about their problems. Most of all, they wanted freedom for the villeins.

ACTIVITY

1 Before you find out what happened in London, it's time to work out why the revolt took place. Below you can see a simple jigsaw. Your task is to fit the six causes of the revolt into the right spaces.

Taxes were collected, including a new Poll Tax.	Freemen hoped for higher wages; villeins wanted freedom.	French attacks on the coast made people angry.	The Black Death led to a huge fall in the population.	Tax collectors set out to find the people who tried to avoid paying the 1380 Poll Tax.	The Statute of Labourers ended the hopes of villeins and freemen.

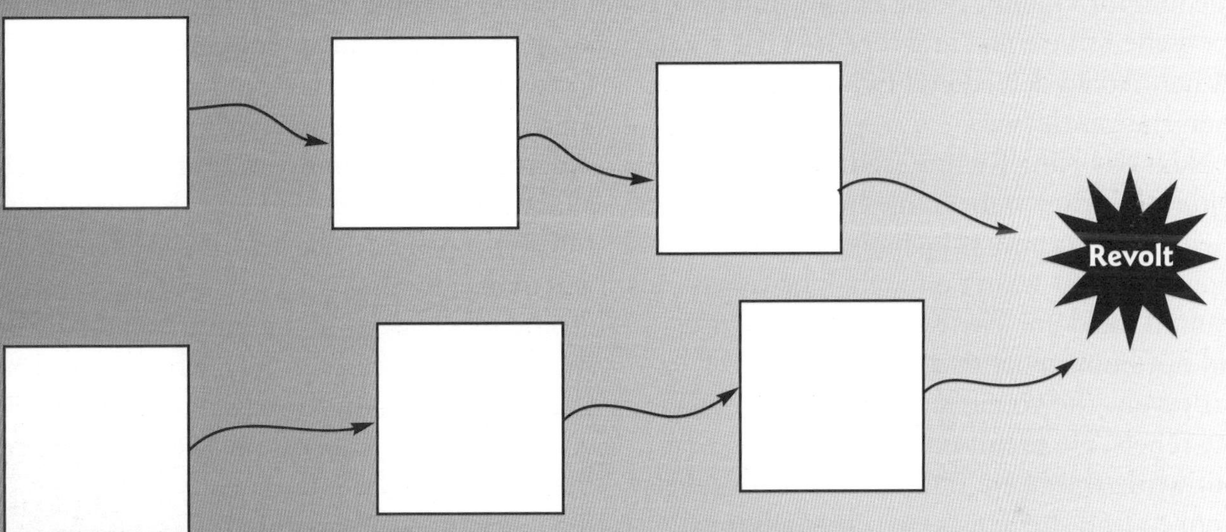

2 Use your finished jigsaw showing the causes of the rebellion to complete a copy of this table. Historians often divide the causes of an event into long-term, medium-term and trigger causes. Which causes of the rebellion go into which sections of this table?

	Causes of the 1381 revolt
Long-term causes (which make an event possible)	
Medium–term causes (which make an event more likely but not inevitable)	
Trigger causes (the events that start a rebellion or a war)	

3 Write a short essay answering this question: 'Why did people rebel in 1381 when they had not rebelled before?' You can get a sheet from your teacher to help you.

What happened during the revolt?

We left the story of the revolt (on page 86) with the rebels, led by Wat Tyler, heading for London. They arrived on 12 June. What would they do next? Burn the city? Kill the King? No. They sent King Richard a message saying that they were loyal to him. They wanted to save him from his treacherous advisers who were ruining the country with taxes. They also demanded higher wages and freedom for villeins. Some even wanted everyone to be equal and repeated the rhyme: 'When Adam delved and Eve span, who was then the gentleman?'

Next day King Richard sent his reply. He said that if they went home he would pardon them of any crimes they had committed. However, that wasn't enough. The rebels wanted freedom. The King and his advisers did not know what to do.

Bravely, the young King rode out to meet the rebels. He promised them their freedom. But while they were talking, a band of rebels went to find the King's two chief advisers, including the Archbishop of Canterbury, and murdered them. After this the revolt became far more violent. Some Londoners joined in, looting houses all over the city.

Next day – 15 June – King Richard went back to speak to Wat Tyler but their talks turned into an argument. The Mayor of London tried to arrest Tyler. Tyler stabbed at the Mayor. The King's knights leaped forward, stabbing at Tyler. He fell from his horse, badly wounded. For a moment it looked as if the rebels would attack the King's men but King Richard rode forward and ordered them to put down their weapons. All along, the protesters had said they were loyal to the King. They obeyed him and the revolt was over.

The rebels went home but they had a shock in store. Early in July, when everything was peaceful again, King Richard went back on his promise. The villeins were not given their freedom. Tyler and nearly 200 other rebel leaders were executed.

Why did villeins win their freedom?

Just a minute! We're investigating how the villeins got their freedom, but the revolt failed. Richard II went back on his word and said they couldn't be free. So how *did* they get their freedom?
Whatever the King said, the revolt had frightened many landowners. They realised that they could not keep people as villeins much longer. Landowners were also still short of workers. If a villein ran away, he could easily find work as a freeman with another landowner. Slowly the landowners freed their villeins. By the mid-1400s nearly everyone was free – at last.
So that's why there aren't any villeins now!

◆ Black Death postscript: a surprising consequence – printing!

Events in history sometimes have obvious and immediate consequences, for example, if there is a war, people are likely to die. But sometimes it takes centuries for an event to lead to changes. And sometimes they lead to changes no one ever dreamed of. Do you know that there is a link between the Black Death and the development of printing? You can work it out from these pictures…

ACTIVITY

The pictures below show some of the changes in the 1400s and 1500s.

1 Put them into the right order so they tell the story of the invention of printing.
2 Divide the consequences of the Black Death into three groups:
   a) short-term consequences
   b) medium-term consequences
   c) long-term consequences.
3 Use the pictures to explain in your own words the link between the Black Death and printing.

In Germany in the 1450s Johannes Gutenberg tried to solve the problem of how to produce books more quickly. He invented a machine that printed books.

After the Black Death there were far fewer workers. Gradually the workers won their freedom and began to earn a lot more money.

The Black Death killed almost half the people of Britain.

They spent their money on more food and better, more colourful, clothes. They also spent money on educating their children.

William Caxton, an English merchant, saw a printing machine and decided to build his own in London. In 1476 he became the first man to print books in England.

More and more people learned to read and write. By the middle of the 1400s about half the people in London could read.

More books were needed but they still had to be written out by hand by people called SCRIVENERS. The scriveners could not keep up with the demand for books.

Printing allowed ideas to travel much more quickly round Europe than ever before.

2.2 WHY HAVE THERE BEEN SO MANY RELIGIOUS CHANGES?

◆ *Why have there been so many religious changes?*

I don't think I'd have liked the 1400s. Free villeins! Printed books! That's too much change for me!
And that's only the beginning. Wait till you hear about religion!
Surely they didn't change religion?
In the 1500s they did...

The Head of the Church
The king or queen was Head of the Church instead of the Pope. This new Church was called the Church of England.

Monasteries
All monasteries were closed. The King and his nobles took the land. Lots of ordinary people who had worked at the monasteries lost their jobs. The monks and nuns no longer provided food, shelter and money to the poor, so the poor got much less help.

Churches
The appearance of churches changed (compare the pictures on pages 18 and 29). Many people did not like the new churches which were less colourful and less friendly.

The Reformation – religious changes in England

Services and the Bible
Services were in English instead of Latin. The Bible was also in English and a copy was put into every church. Now more people could read the Bible and think about religion for themselves. Before this they had depended on what the priests told them.

Holy days and holidays
People had to stop celebrating saints' days and other Catholic holy days. This meant they had fewer holidays and celebrations. Parish churches were used just for services instead of for celebrations and holidays.

ACTIVITY A

1 Look at the churches on pages 18 and 29. List the differences. Think about the decoration and the priest.

2 Which of the changes in the above diagram do you think was most important to ordinary people?

3 Which of the changes do you think was most important to the King and his nobles?

Sir Geoffrey Luttrell: *Those changes are terrible. What was wrong with the old ways?*

Flora Thompson: *Some people said nothing was wrong. They liked the old Church. But others said the Catholic Church had gone wrong. They started their own Churches. Because they were protesting about the Catholic Church they were called Protestants. These Protestants were led by Martin Luther, a German priest. And because they were trying to reform the Church this movement was called the Reformation.*

The Catholic Church is too rich. The bishops are only interested in becoming richer. They have forgotten about Jesus Christ helping the poor.

Services should not be in Latin. They should be in a language the people can understand. Then they will understand religion and have a better chance of going to Heaven when they die.

The bishops spend too much time with kings and not enough time praying and spreading their religion. Let the people choose their own priests and do away with bishops.

Churches should be simple places. Do away with all the colours and rich furnishings so that the people can concentrate on the word of God.

Martin Luther's ideas

These Protestants were in a minority. But they were powerful, especially in London, and these new ideas were spreading fast, thanks to printing. Books spread ideas much more quickly than any man could by riding round on his horse talking to people.

ACTIVITY B

Henry had his new title added to all the new coins produced. It is still there on English coins today. Can you find it?

Flora Thompson: *When Henry VIII became King of England he heard about these ideas. He hated them. He even wrote a book condemning them. The Pope gave him a special title: Fidei Defensor, or Defender of the Faith.*

Sir Geoffrey Luttrell: *Henry sounds like a good man. So who's the guilty person who changed the Church?*

Flora Thompson: *Are you ready for a shock . . . ?*

◆ Why did Henry VIII change the Church?

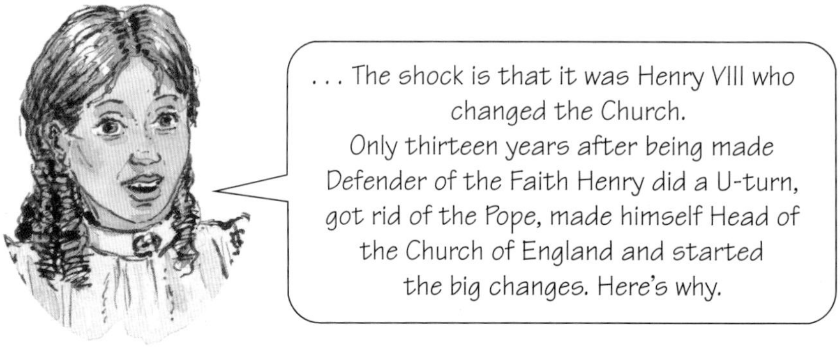

... The shock is that it was Henry VIII who changed the Church. Only thirteen years after being made Defender of the Faith Henry did a U-turn, got rid of the Pope, made himself Head of the Church of England and started the big changes. Here's why.

Unravelling the mystery of Henry's U-turn

Henry VIII had two big problems.

1 He wanted a son who could be King after he died, but his wife Catherine was growing old and seemed unlikely to have a healthy son.

I want a son, not a daughter. Only a son can rule England after I die.

2 He was also running short of money.

All your wars and rich living have left you bankrupt I am afraid.

3 Henry asked the Pope for a divorce from Catherine so he could marry Anne Boleyn. He was certain she'd have a son.

4 But the Pope refused. Catherine was a loyal Catholic; Anne believed in the new Protestant ideas.

No!

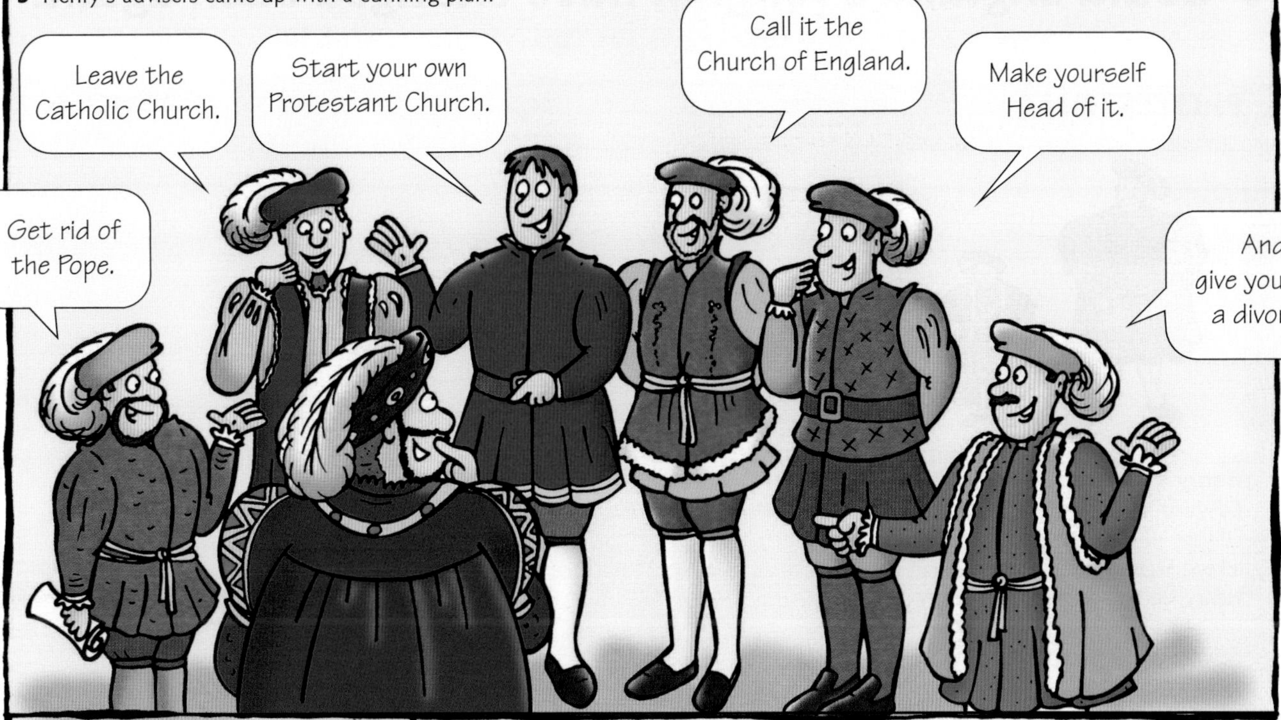

5 Henry's advisers came up with a cunning plan.

Get rid of the Pope.

Leave the Catholic Church.

Start your own Protestant Church.

Call it the Church of England.

Make yourself Head of it.

And . . . give yourself a divorce!

6 So that's what he did.

I hereby grant myself a divorce.

7 And three years later he found the plan could solve his money problems too. He closed the monasteries and took away all their land.

Sir Geoffrey Luttrell: *So in one way this Reformation thing happened because of Henry's personal problems. It had nothing to do with Luther's ideas (see page 91) at all.*

Samuel Pepys: *But in another way that's not quite true. Henry was a Catholic but his advisers and Anne Boleyn herself were all Protestants. It wasn't an accident that they came up with their plan. They wanted a Protestant Church. It solved Henry's problems but it solved theirs too.*

Flora Thompson: *Things did not change overnight but England steadily became more Protestant. Catholics who tried to keep the old ways were imprisoned and sometimes tortured or executed.*

ACTIVITY

Fill in a copy of this table with any evidence you can find to support either theory.

Theory 1: Henry changed the Church to solve his own political problems	Theory 2: Henry changed the Church because he liked Protestant ways better than Catholic ones

◆ Could England's religion have changed back again?

PROTESTANT

Henry VIII (ruled 1509–1547)
Edward VI (ruled 1547–1553)
Edward VI was Henry's son. He was a keen Protestant, far more so than Henry, and made sure the country remained Protestant. However, Edward died when he was only 16.

Mary Tudor (ruled 1553–1558)
Mary was Henry VIII's eldest daughter. She was a Catholic like her mother, Catherine of Aragon. When she became Queen she changed the country's religion back to being Catholic. About 280 Protestants were burnt at the stake for refusing to become Catholics. However many people were glad to be Catholic again. They had missed the colourful churches and services. Mary died when she was only 42. She had no children so her sister Elizabeth became Queen.

Elizabeth I (ruled 1558–1603)
Elizabeth was a Protestant. She also wanted as many people as possible to be united and support her as Queen. She believed that there would be fewer problems if the country was Protestant than if it was Catholic, so she changed the country's religion back to being Protestant. Many people were still secret Catholics, especially in the north of England. However, she did not execute anyone who disagreed, so long as they did not rebel against her. Elizabeth was Queen for over 40 years and people became so used to being Protestant that by the time she died they could not remember another religion.

ACTIVITY A

1. Why did Mary change the religion?
2. Why did it change back after Mary's death?
3. Was it inevitable that England was still a Protestant country in 1600?
4. Why did kings and queens think it was important for everyone to have the same religion (see page 95)?

Why did everyone have to believe the same thing?

One of the hardest things to understand looking back at this period is why, when the king or queen changed religion, everyone had to change. Nowadays we see religion as a purely personal matter. It is up to each individual to decide what to believe. We say it is a matter of conscience. Some would say it does not matter what you believe. In the 1500s it was different. You had to believe what the monarch told you to.

Why were kings and queens so keen that everyone followed the same religion? There were different answers to this question at different times.

Answer A

It's dangerous for the whole country to have different religions. The country should be united. Everyone has to support the king or queen. You can't have some people putting the Pope and their religion before their loyalty to the king or queen. Look what happened in 1588 when the Pope and the King of Spain sent the Spanish Armada to conquer England. They wanted to make England Catholic again – by force. If a lot of English people had supported the Pope instead of Queen Elizabeth then the Armada might have been successful.

Answer B

We believe that there is only one true religion. If you follow the wrong beliefs then you will go to Hell instead of going to Heaven. So the king or queen must protect the people by making sure that they all follow the right religion and go to Heaven.

SOURCE 1 The Spanish Armada of 1588 shown as a huge dragon threatening England.

SOURCE 2 A group of heretics being burned at the stake because they would not accept the country's religion.

ACTIVITY B

1 a) Which of our time travellers might have given Answer A to explain why everyone had to follow the same religion?

b) Explain why you chose that person.

2 a) Which of our time travellers might have given Answer B?

b) Why did you choose that person?

◆ How were people of different religions treated?

ACTIVITY

Attitudes to religion have changed a great deal over the centuries. On this page are seven boxes which tell you how people have treated those who have different religious beliefs from them.

1 Put the boxes into chronological order.
2 Draw a timeline showing the years 1000–2000 and write the box numbers on the correct dates. You will have to do some research for this.
3 Do you think that attitudes to people of different religions changed **a)** very slowly **b)** steadily **c)** quickly? Explain your answer, using evidence from boxes 1–7.
4 Why do you think people have become more tolerant of different religions?

1 Protestants burned
Nearly 300 Protestants were burned to death during the reign of Mary Tudor. Mary wanted everyone to become Catholic again. Protestant leaders were burned as punishment and to persuade others to become Catholics.

2 Equal rights for Catholics
For over 200 years only members of the Church of England were allowed to vote and become MPs. This finally changed in the early 1800s when Catholics and other religious groups were given the right to vote and become MPs. They were no longer second-class citizens.

3 The Crusades
Richard I, the great leader of the Crusades. In Richard's time wars were fought against Muslims for control of Jerusalem and other holy places. Knights were expected to fight against people who were not Christians.

4 Multi-faith Britain
Most British cities now have mosques, temples and places of worship for many religions as well as Christianity.

5 Intolerance
From Flora Thompson, *Lark Rise to Candleford*.

To Catholics the Lark Rise people were intolerant. People who were not religious themselves became quite heated when the Catholics were mentioned. On Sundays the children would see horses and traps loaded with families on their way to the Catholic church and they ran after them shouting 'Old Catholics! Old lick the cats!'

6 The Pilgrim Fathers
The Pilgrim Fathers sailed to America on the *Mayflower* during the reign of James I. They were not allowed to hold church services in the way they wanted to so they left for America where they could have freedom to worship God in their own way.

7 The expulsion of the Jews
Jews were expelled from England in the reign of Edward I. They were not allowed to return for over 300 years, until 1655 when Oliver Cromwell ruled England.

2.3 WHY DID PEOPLE MOVE TO TOWNS?

Sir Geoffrey Luttrell: *Now for our third and final puzzle. In my time nearly everyone lived in the country and worked as farmers. Now all that's changed. Most people seem to live in towns.*

Flora Thompson: *It's all because of the Industrial Revolution. People left farming to work in manufacturing industries and that meant moving to towns, where the factories were. That all happened between about 1750 and 1900. It wasn't a sudden change but it was a very big one – that's why it's called a revolution.*

Samuel Pepys: *Tell me more about this revolution…*

ACTIVITY

Use Source 1 to discuss these questions. Don't worry if you're not sure – just think of possible explanations at this stage.

1 Which region had the most large towns in 1550?
2 Why do you think this region had large towns?
3 Which region had the largest towns in 1900?
4 Why do you think this region had large towns?

SOURCE 1 The largest British towns in 1550 and 1900.

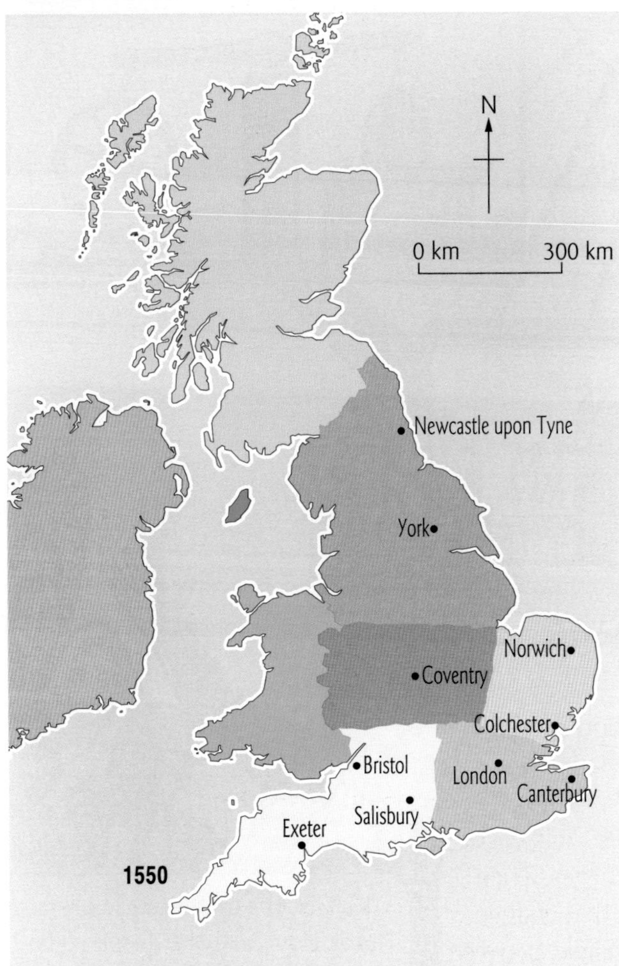

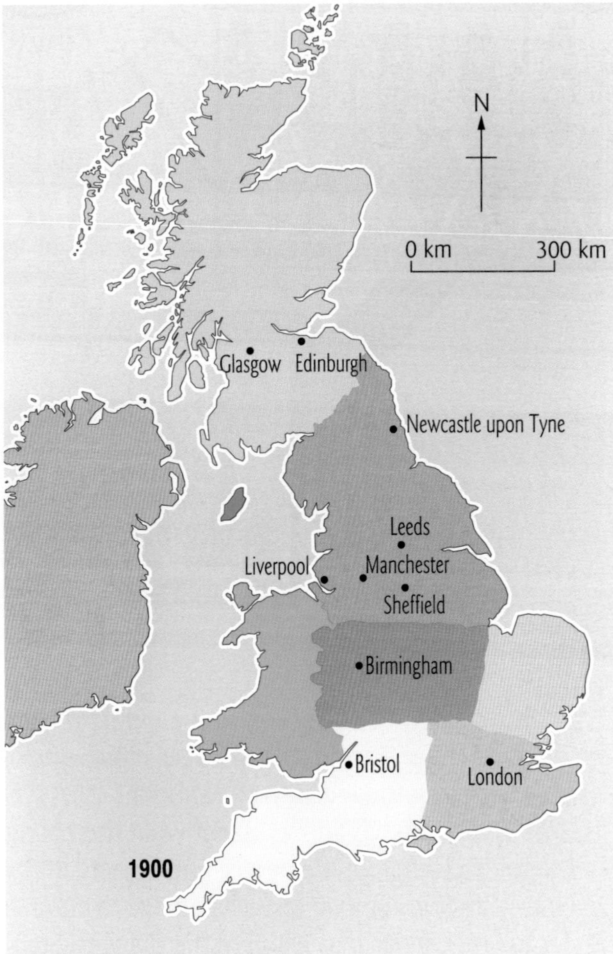

◆ Roll up, roll up for the Industrial Revolution!

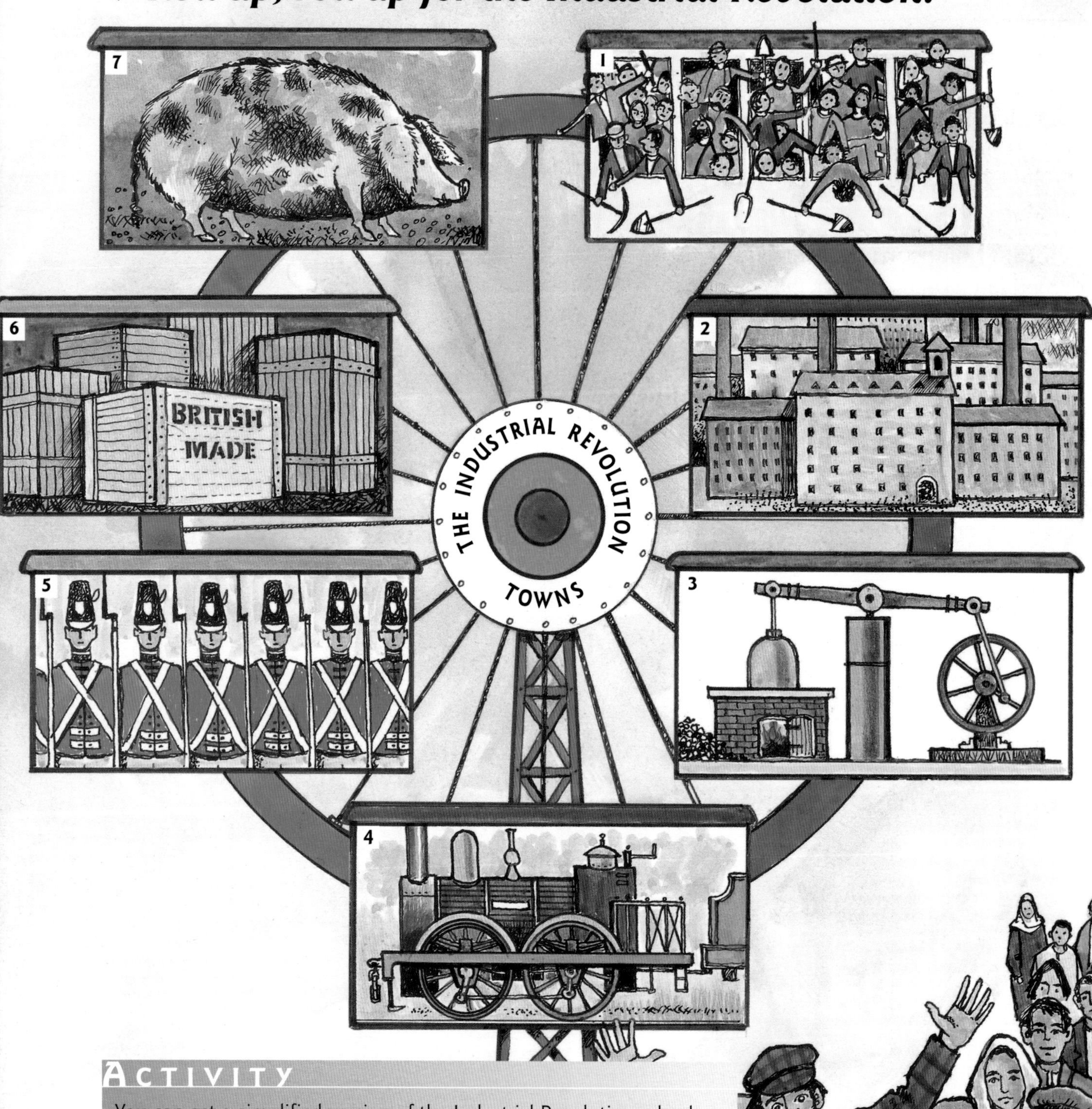

ACTIVITY

You can get a simplified version of the Industrial Revolution wheel from your teacher. Each of the carriages represents one change that happened during the Industrial Revolution.

1 Read pages 99–103 and work out what the changes are. You might get some clues from the people and objects in the carriages. Then write a title on the side of each carriage to summarise that change.
2 Try to find connections between the changes. Start with links between **a)** changes 3 and 4 **b)** changes 1 and 7 **c)** any other changes.

Roll up, roll up for the Industrial Revolution! Join the queue to find a job in the towns. Don't get left behind in the countryside.

Carriage 1

The population was growing. Between 1700 and 1900 the population of Britain became four times as big, as you can see from Source 2.

Large families always need more things – clothes, furniture, cups and pans, cutlery, even toys for the children.
I can employ more people in my factory. More and more people want the clothes we make so I need more workers to keep up with demand.

SOURCE 2 How the population of Britain increased between 1700 and 1901.

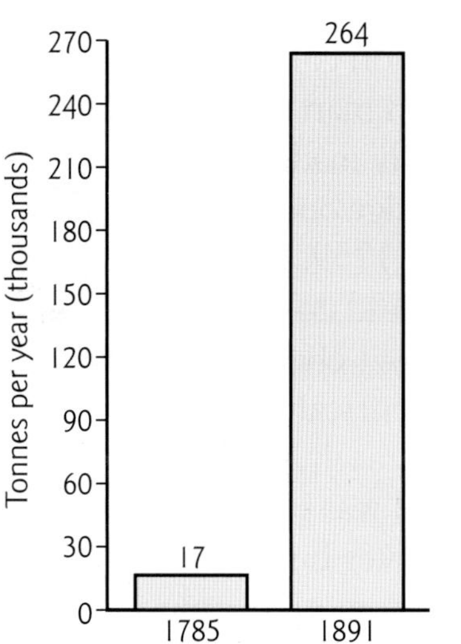

SOURCE 3 The increase in the production of soap between 1785 and 1891.

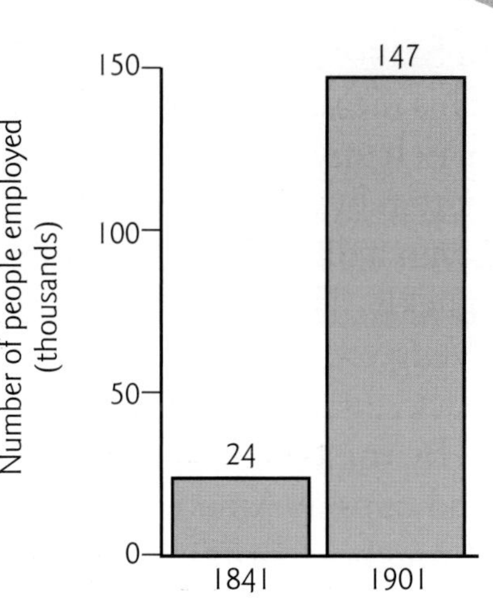

SOURCE 4 The number of people employed in the chemicals, oil and soap industries.

Carriage 2

More, more, more! People wanted more clothes, more furniture, more everything. How could the supply keep up with this demand? The answer was that businesses invented new ways of doing things which were quicker; cheaper; better. Mass production was beginning.

Example 1: Cotton

Until the 1750s most cloth was made in people's own homes (see Source 5). Women spun the wool or cotton into thread and then both men and women wove the thread into cloth. However, as demand for cloth rose, this 'Domestic System' could not keep up. Inventors invented machines to make cloth more quickly. These machines needed factories to go in. Gradually more and more cloth was made in factories (Source 6), where large numbers of workers used machines to make cloth more quickly and more cheaply.

SOURCE 5 The domestic system.

SOURCE 6 A factory interior.

Example 2: Pottery

For centuries, there had been hundreds of small workshops making cups, pots and vases in the region called 'The Potteries' in Staffordshire. In the workshops each man made a whole pot. This meant that each item was carefully made but it didn't match anything else! Then Josiah Wedgwood changed this system by setting up his first factory in 1759. Each worker was given a different task that he or she could do repeatedly – and quickly. The result was higher quality yet cheaper pottery. Wedgwood's dishes and plates were identical so they could be stacked safely. His teapots poured accurately, every time!

By the end of the 1700s Wedgwood was selling his plates and cups in America, Russia and all over Europe as well as throughout Britain. There were always more people wanting to buy his goods. As a result Wedgwood needed to employ more people in his factories to keep up with the demand. Most other pottery makers had to copy his methods in order to compete. It was a similar story in nearly all industries.

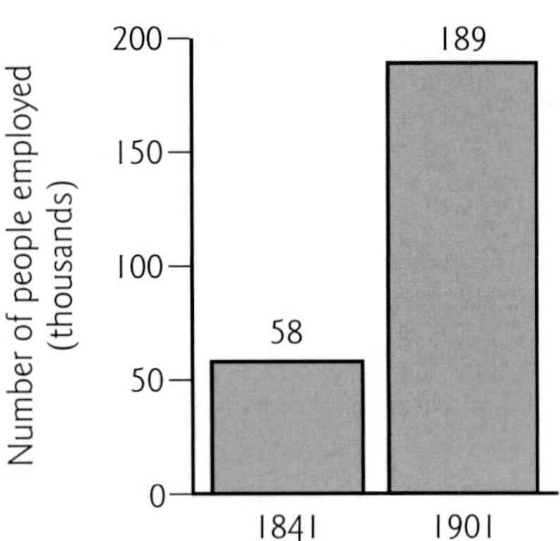

SOURCE 7 This graph shows the number of people employed in the pottery and glass industries.

Carriage 3

SOURCE 8 A steam engine used to draw coal in a Staffordshire colliery, early 1800s.

Before 1700 the main forms of power were:

- human power (e.g. a person pedalling a spinning wheel)
- horse power (e.g. a horse-drawn plough)
- wind power (e.g. a windmill grinding corn)
- water power (e.g. a water wheel)

In the 1800s a big change occurred. The steam engine became the main form of power.

Since the early 1700s steam engines had been used to pump water out of coal mines. In 1765 James Watt invented an improved steam engine which used less coal. Together with Matthew Boulton he built and sold steam engines and by the mid-1800s steam engines powered the iron and steel industries, drove ships, hauled coal from mines, drove farm machinery and powered the machines which made the cloth in the cotton factories. The steam engine was the heart of the Industrial Revolution. All this had a big effect on where the factories were built. The *only* place to build a steam-powered factory was on a coalfield, or as near to the coal as possible. The north and midlands had plenty of coal. The new big towns in Source 1 on page 97 were all near coal deposits. The new steam engine also provided lots more jobs for coal miners. In the 1800s the number of miners increased by twenty times.

Carriage 4

Steam power also helped to lead to one of the biggest changes of all – the development of the railways. In 1830 the first steam-powered railway was built between Liverpool and Manchester. This was followed by a railway boom. In the 1840s and 1850s railway lines and stations were built throughout the country. By 1851 65,000 people worked on the railways in jobs that had not existed before, such as engine drivers, porters, clerks and messengers. Businesses transported their goods more cheaply *and* more quickly than before. Trains allowed commuters to travel from suburbs to their work in the centre of towns. Seaside towns like Scarborough grew as trains brought in more and more holidaymakers.

SOURCE 9 A train on the Liverpool and Manchester Railway, 1833. This train had open second-class carriages to transport ordinary people.

Carriage 5

War helped industry to grow. For 22 years, from 1793 to 1815, Britain was at war with France. Sources 10 and 11 show two of the most famous battles of that war. This war kept the iron industry busy producing weapons and ammunition for the army and navy. It also kept ship builders busy making ships. The war helped these industries grow. It gave jobs to lots of people.

After the war ended these arms manufacturers and ship builders did not close down. They had to carry on supplying the army and the navy who were needed to build and defend Britain's empire, but they also expanded into making other things that Britain wanted at home, such as rails for the railways and ships for British merchants. More workers were needed.

SOURCE 10 Victory for Britain at the Battle of Trafalgar in 1805 made Britain safe from invasion by France. It also ensured that Britain's navy was the most powerful in the world throughout the 1800s.

SOURCE 11 Victory for Britain at the Battle of Waterloo in 1815 ended the war between Britain and France.

Carriage 6

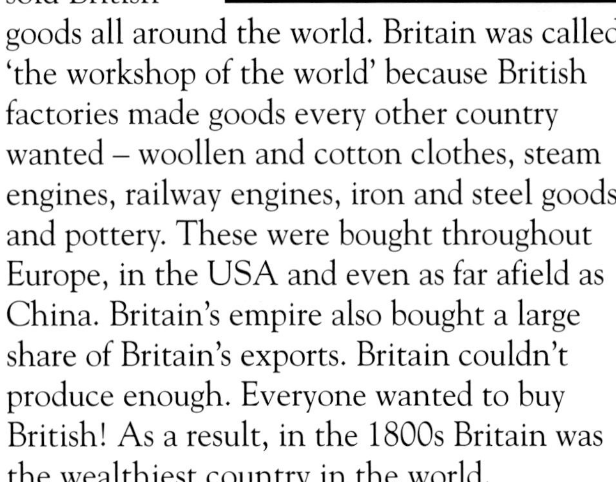

British traders sold British goods all around the world. Britain was called 'the workshop of the world' because British factories made goods every other country wanted – woollen and cotton clothes, steam engines, railway engines, iron and steel goods and pottery. These were bought throughout Europe, in the USA and even as far afield as China. Britain's empire also bought a large share of Britain's exports. Britain couldn't produce enough. Everyone wanted to buy British! As a result, in the 1800s Britain was the wealthiest country in the world.

SOURCE 12 This is a map of the British Empire (shown in orange) at its peak in the late 1800s.

Carriage 7

Farming was changing. During the 1700s the weight of the sheep sold at market trebled. The amount of corn grown per acre increased by over 40 per cent. This great improvement was deliberate and is called the Agricultural Revolution. More food was being produced because of new inventions and improved farming methods. However, these new methods did not mean more jobs. In fact farmers were developing better equipment, and machines were slowly replacing farmworkers, especially in the later 1800s. To make matters worse for farmworkers, it was just at this time that the population of villages was growing most rapidly. Many young farmworkers headed for the towns to earn better money to feed their families.

So, you see, there are lots of reasons why people moved to the towns.

There usually are lots of reasons for something happening in history. You shouldn't just find one reason and think that's all there is to it.

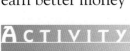

You are now going to think about how all these changes led to the big change we started with: 'Why did people move to towns?'

1 Draw a second large wheel diagram.
2 Write the word 'towns' in the centre – at the hub of the wheel.
3 Write your seven 'change' headings around the rim.
4 Now draw spokes between the rim and the hub explaining **why** this change made people move to towns. Each spoke should show one reason why people moved. There will be more spokes from some changes to others. You might not be able to think of spokes for all the changes.

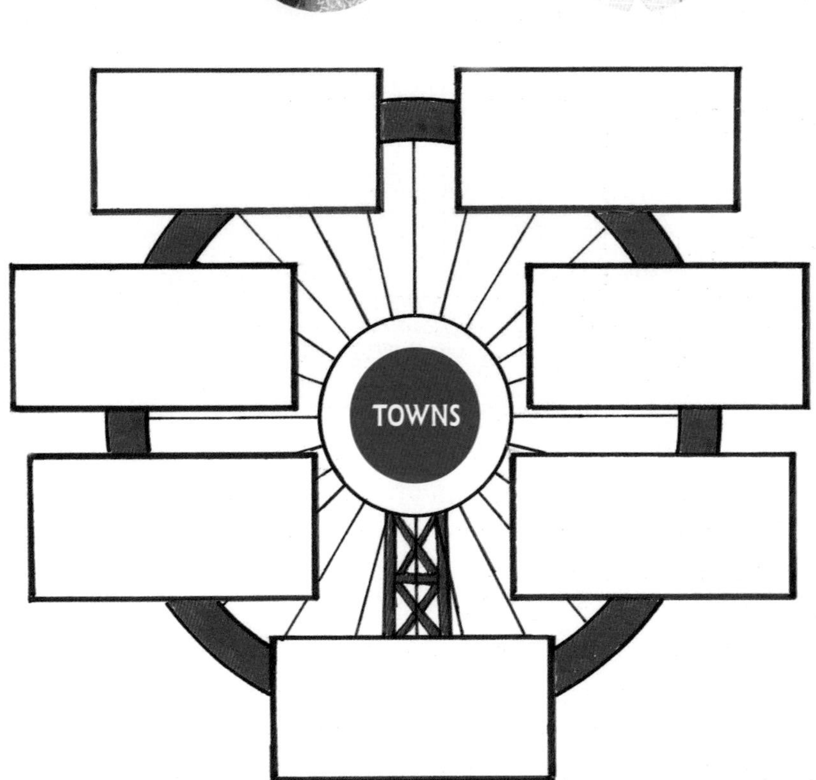

◆ *What was it like to live in the new industrial towns?*

SOURCE 13 An engraving highlighting the poor conditions in the slum areas of London.

There were many jobs but the workers had to work ten or twelve hours a day. They did not have time to walk miles to and from work so houses were built close to the factories. They were crammed close together, without light or fresh water supplies.

As the towns grew, the conditions got worse. Town councils could collect taxes to pay for clean water and sewers but most decided against taxing the wealthy to improve conditions for the poor. In the 1840s Friedrich Engels described how the poorest labourers in Manchester lived:

Heaps of refuse, offal and sickening filth are everywhere. A horde of ragged women and children swarm about the streets and they are just as dirty as the pigs which wallow happily in the heaps of garbage and the pools of filth. On average twenty people live in these little houses of two rooms, an attic and a cellar. One toilet is shared by 120 people.

ACTIVITY

1 Read the information above. Make a list of the problems for poor people living in towns.
2 Read page 105. How did people try to get improvements in their living conditions?
3 Read page 106. Give two reasons why changes were made.

Outdoor workers, like builders and brick-makers, had no work in winter. If an 'ill-wind' kept ships out of the port then dockers could not earn any money. There was no help from the government for the poor and jobless unless they gave up their homes and went into the workhouse, where families were split up, wore workhouse clothes and were made to feel like criminals. Most people struggled on to avoid the workhouse, living on potatoes and tea made from tea-leaves already used once in the homes of wealthier families.

Food could be dangerous. Some shopkeepers mixed chalk into bread, and copper or turnips into jam to save money. Water came from sewers often full of dead fish, cats and dogs. Diseases raged through the towns. Cholera and typhoid killed people in their thousands. In 1848 *The Times* newspaper printed a letter:

Sur,
May we beg and beseech your proteckshion. We live in muck and filthe. We aint got no privez, no dustbins, no water supplies, no drain or suer in the whole place. We al of us suffer and numbers are ill and if the Cholera comes lord help us.

◆ *How did people try to improve their towns?*

In the early 1800s only 11 per cent of men and no women could vote in elections for Members of Parliament. Therefore no ordinary people had a say in who was in the government which made the laws. In fact, the big industrial towns did not even elect MPs to Parliament. If people wanted to call for change, the usual way to do it was to riot.

Riots

Most riots were not wild, chaotic events where people did whatever they wanted. Most riots had leaders who stayed in control and tried to organise their followers.

High food prices were commonly a reason for riots. High prices were a result of bad harvests. When food prices increased, people feared starvation and became desperate. A good example took place in Carlisle in 1811. Three hundred men and women broke into some warehouses and began to carry off all the food they could find. The government sent in the army to stop them. Stones were thrown at the soldiers. The soldiers fired back. One woman was killed and several were wounded.

Protest meetings

Other 'riots' were more like what we would call 'protests' today. But the government still called them riots and clamped down hard. There were no police then, so soldiers were sent in to break up the protests. The reason for this was that the government and all the landowners were afraid of a revolution starting in Britain. They had watched in horror in the 1790s as the French Revolution led to the execution of the King of France and many nobles. They feared that if they gave in to any of the rioters' demands then the people would think the government was weak and this would encourage them to revolt. Therefore they did not give in to any of the demands for better conditions. For example, in 1819 60,000 people went to a meeting at St Peter's Fields in Manchester (see Source 14). They were demanding the right to vote. They hoped that if they could vote, then the politicians would have to listen to their complaints about life in the towns. When the peaceful meeting was broken up by soldiers, eleven people were killed and 400 were wounded. The event became known as 'Peterloo', a reference to the Battle of Waterloo four years earlier.

SOURCE 14 The riot at Peterloo.

◆ *When did life in the towns improve?*

In 1832 the government did listen and made a new law, the Reform Act, which

a) gave some of the rapidly growing industrial towns their own MPs for the first time. These included Leeds, Manchester and Birmingham

b) allowed middle-class men in the towns to vote. However, the working people who lived in the terrible houses and disease-filled streets still could not vote.

Charters

After this small success the ordinary people tried a new way of winning the vote. They got as many people as possible to sign a petition or 'charter', demanding the vote. They were called Chartists. Three times they handed in charters signed by millions of people but still the government would not give them the vote.

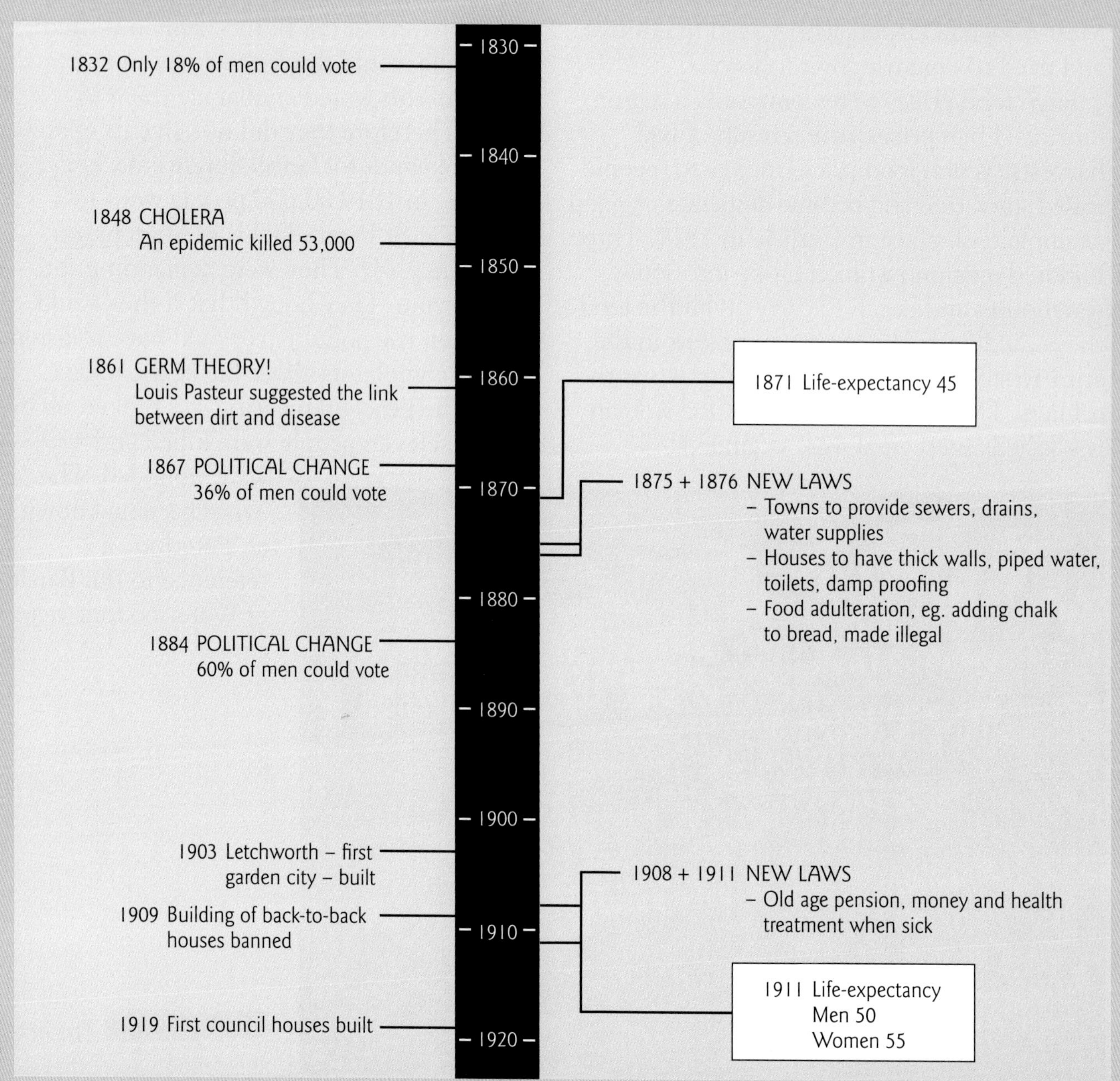
1830
1832 Only 18% of men could vote
1840
1848 CHOLERA
An epidemic killed 53,000
1850
1861 GERM THEORY!
Louis Pasteur suggested the link between dirt and disease
1860
1871 Life-expectancy 45
1867 POLITICAL CHANGE
36% of men could vote
1870
1875 + 1876 NEW LAWS
– Towns to provide sewers, drains, water supplies
– Houses to have thick walls, piped water, toilets, damp proofing
– Food adulteration, eg. adding chalk to bread, made illegal
1880
1884 POLITICAL CHANGE
60% of men could vote
1890
1900
1903 Letchworth – first garden city – built
1908 + 1911 NEW LAWS
– Old age pension, money and health treatment when sick
1909 Building of back-to-back houses banned
1910
1911 Life-expectancy
Men 50
Women 55
1919 First council houses built
1920

◆ *Why was the Industrial Revolution so important?*

The Industrial Revolution was the biggest change in our history. Since the beginning of time most people had lived by farming. After the Industrial Revolution most people earned their living by working in manufacturing industries or other businesses. Only a minority lived by farming.

And there was something else that was special happening in the 1700s, at the beginning of the Industrial Revolution. Can you work out what it was from these three graphs?

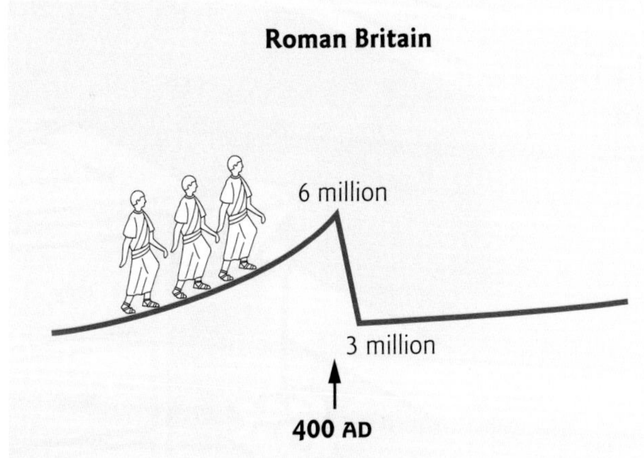

Around 400AD and again in the 1340s the population of Britain fell drastically. The population had risen, then starvation or disease brought it back down. It was as if Britain could only support a certain amount of people.

In the 1700s the population was rising again. Some people predicted that the same would happen as in the past: that starvation or disease would kill off millions of people. They said Britain could not feed this growing population. They were wrong, as you can see from the graph for the 1700s below.

Twice before, the population of Britain had been halved by starvation and disease, but in the 1700s the revolutions in farming and industry meant that there was enough food and money to keep people alive, so the population kept rising instead of falling back again.

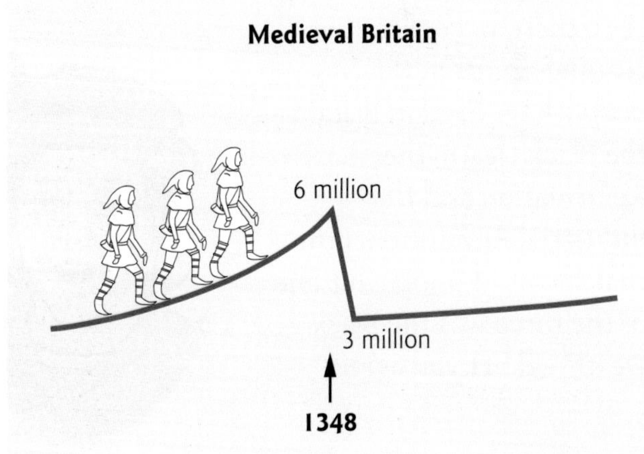

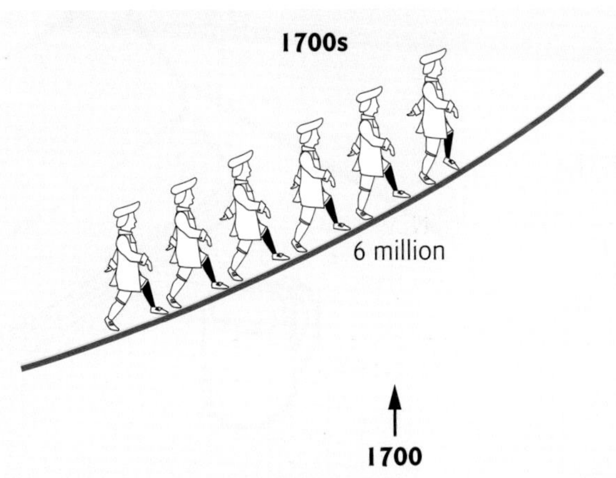

2.4 CONCLUSION

Think about what you have learned from your travels through time

◆ What have you learned . . . about everyday life?

History according to Sir Geoffrey

I'm glad I stowed away on your time capsule. I've certainly learned a lot about how life changed over the centuries. The villeins won their freedom after the Black Death in the 1600s, at the time of the Civil War. Religion changed too in the Reformation. That was when Queen Elizabeth married Oliver Cromwell and began the Church of England. Most people carried on working as farmers until the 1800s. Then they moved into towns and began working in factories. That was after the invention of computers. We call that change the Industrial Revolution.

So there were three big turning-points in the way people have lived in Britain – the Black Death, the Reformation and the Industrial Revolution. I think that the most important one of the three was the Black Death – don't you agree?

ACTIVITY A

1 On your own copy of Sir Geoffrey's summary
   a) mark in blue all the statements in the first paragraph that you think are accurate.
   b) mark in red all the statements in the first paragraph that you think are wrong.
2 Rewrite the summary correcting Sir Geoffrey's mistakes.
3 Sir Geoffrey says that the Black Death was the most important turning-point in the way we have lived in Britain. Explain why you agree or disagree with him.

As you travelled through time you learned a lot about the changes in the way people lived. Sir Geoffrey Luttrell showed you life in the Middle Ages, Samuel Pepys told you about Stuart England and Flora Thompson described her life in Victorian England. You must now feel like a real expert in the history of everyday life.

The next activity gives you the chance to test your knowledge. How many of the questions below do you know the answer to? Don't worry – you don't have to answer them again. It's your chance to realise just how much you have learned. There may be some questions here that you can't answer yet – but you will be able to, once you have studied other periods of history.

ACTIVITY B

Look at the picture.

1 Which questions can you answer after working on this book?

2 Which questions remain unanswered?

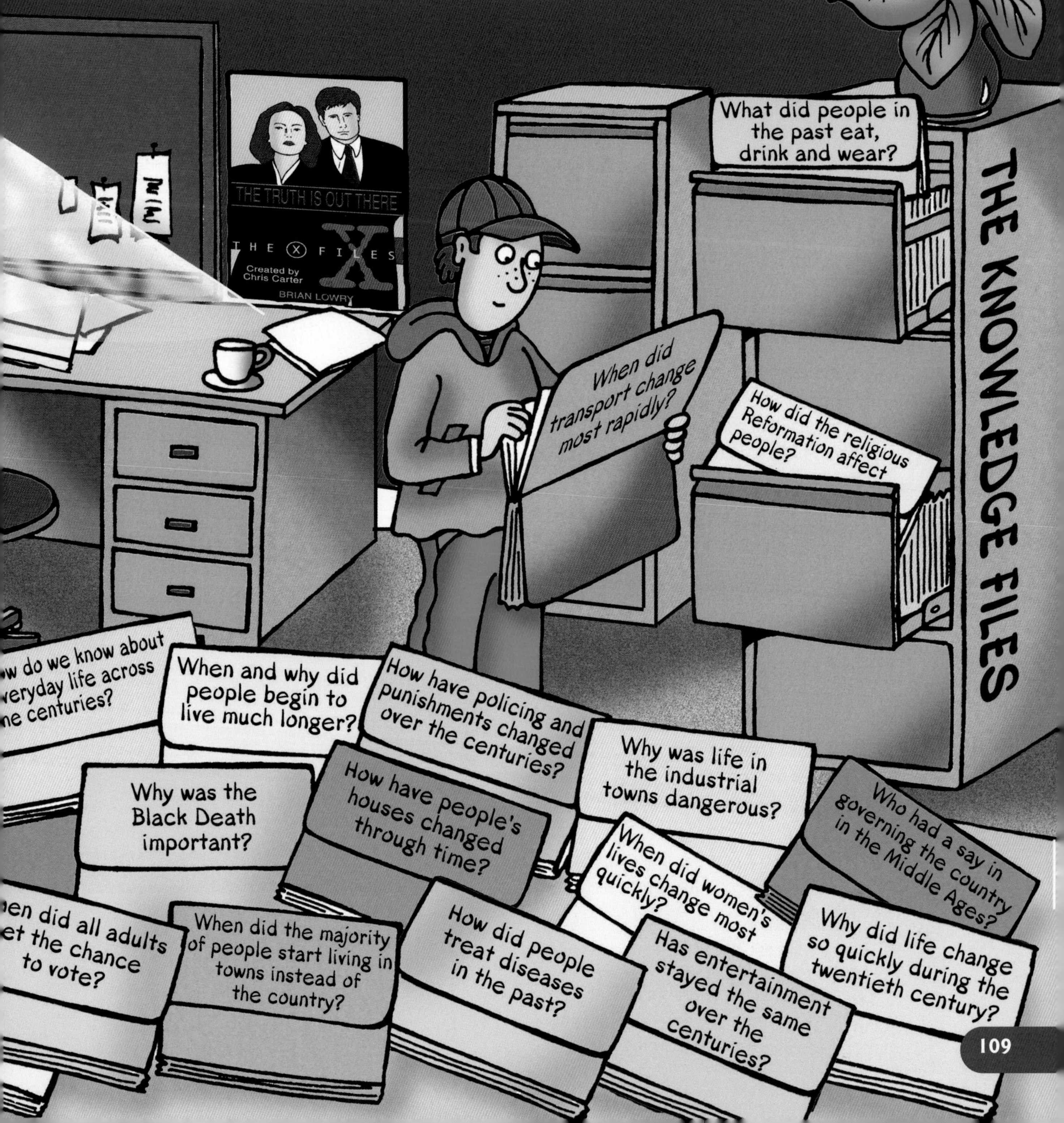

THE TRUTH IS OUT THERE
THE X FILES
Created by Chris Carter
BRIAN LOWRY
THE KNOWLEDGE FILES
What did people in the past eat, drink and wear?
When did transport change most rapidly?
How did the religious Reformation affect people?
w do we know about veryday life across ne centuries?
When and why did people begin to live much longer?
How have policing and punishments changed over the centuries?
Why was life in the industrial towns dangerous?
Who had a say in governing the country in the Middle Ages?
Why was the Black Death important?
How have people's houses changed through time?
When did women's lives change most quickly?
Why did life change so quickly during the twentieth century?
en did all adults et the chance to vote?
When did the majority of people start living in towns instead of the country?
How did people treat diseases in the past?
Has entertainment stayed the same over the centuries?

◆ What have you learned . . . about historical sources?

While you travelled in time you did not just learn about how people lived their lives. You also learned about the sources that tell us about the past. You discovered the drawings in the Luttrell Psalter, the diary of Samuel Pepys and Flora Thompson's autobiography *Lark Rise to Candleford*. Pictures, diaries and books are just three types of sources that give us evidence about the past but there are lots more sources, as you can see on this timeline.

Buildings and furniture

Histories and religious books written by monks

Letters by v

Wills and inventories – lists of possessions

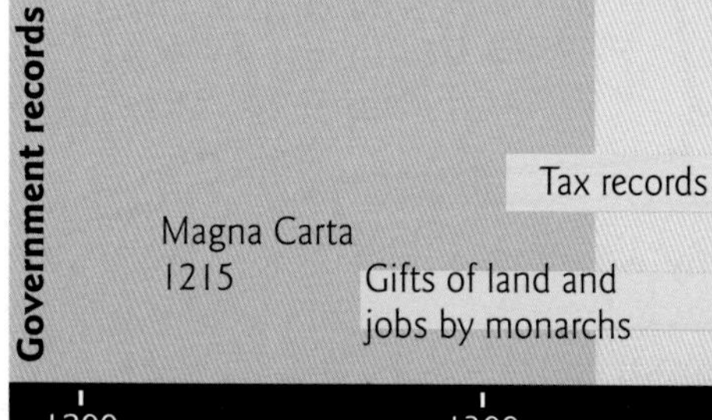

Government records

Tax records

Magna Carta 1215

Gifts of land and jobs by monarchs

1200 1300 1400

WHO DO WE KNOW ABOUT?

Kings, queens, nobles and wealthy families

ACTIVITY

1 Which of these statements are TRUE and which are FALSE? Explain your answers.

a) The speeches of the Luttrell villagers were invented by the writer of this book but were based on real events.

b) Only the Luttrell family in the medieval village were real people. The rest are fictional.

c) The words of Samuel Pepys are really his. They are not fiction.

d) Flora Thompson's description of her childhood was invented by the writer of this book.

2 If you want to discover more about the Luttrells, Pepys and Flora Thompson, which other sources would you use to find out about each of them?

3 Choose two of the sources below and explain why they

a) are valuable for finding out about the past

b) need to be checked before you can believe what they say.

letters	diaries	photographs	newspapers

4 Why is it harder to find out about the lives of ordinary people in the Middle Ages than about ordinary people in the Victorian period?

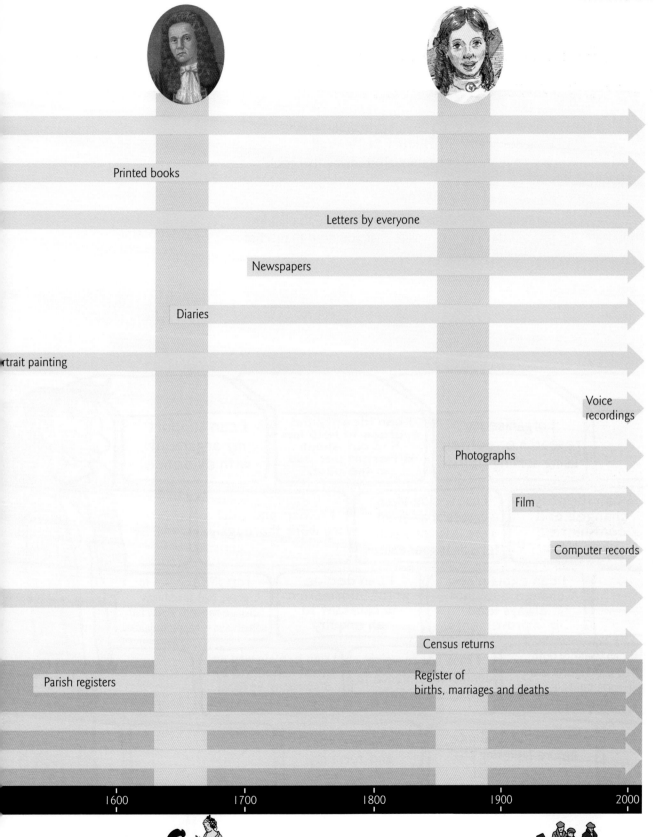

Printed books

Letters by everyone

Newspapers

Diaries

rtrait painting

Voice recordings

Photographs

Film

Computer records

Census returns

Parish registers

Register of births, marriages and deaths

1600 1700 1800 1900 2000

Still know far more about rich than poor

More records about everybody – rich and poor

◆ *What have you learned . . . about historical skills?*

ACTIVITY

The Activities in this book have been designed to improve your historical skills. Look carefully at the **History Skills Wall**.

1 Which new skills have you learned through studying this book?
2 Which skills have you improved?
3 Which skills do you need to develop further?
4 Before your next unit of work in history, design an action plan for yourself. Set yourself three targets – skills that you need to practise to improve your work in history.

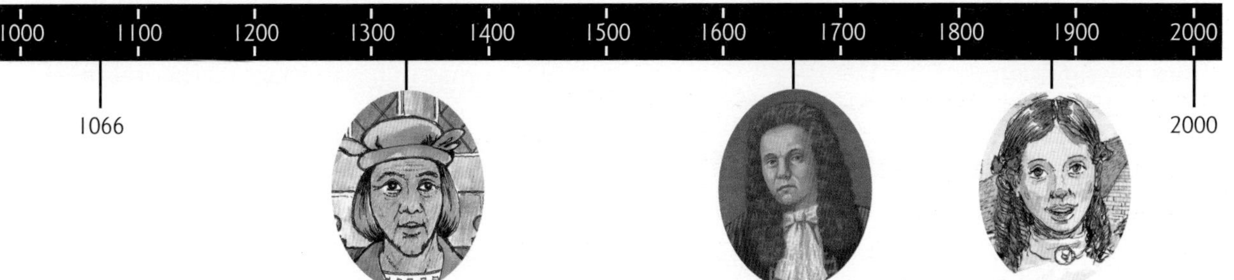

It's time for us to go home. We hope you enjoyed your adventure, time-travelling through history. Next time you start a history topic think about us and work out when the new topic fits – was it in the Middle Ages before Sir Geoffrey? Or between Sir Geoffrey and Samuel in Tudor and Stuart times? Or between Samuel and Flora (that's me!) as the Industrial Revolution was beginning?
Use us as a living timeline and fill in the gaps as you study more history. We hope you enjoy it!

◆ Glossary

BALTIC the sea between northern Germany and Russia. Merchants bought timber, fish and furs from the lands around the Baltic

BLEEDING opening a vein and letting blood flow out of the body. This was done to restore the balance of the humours in the body

BREECHES trousers

CANDLEMAS a church festival on 2nd February when candles were lit to celebrate the beginning of Spring

DYKES low turf walls to protect the land from flooding

FALLOW leaving a field empty so that no crops grow. This helps the soil recover so that the crop is better the next year

GARDEROBE a toilet

HERETICS people who refused to agree with the beliefs of the Church. They were often executed by burning to frighten other people away from questioning the Church

HOLY LAND the area around Jerusalem that now includes Israel, Palestine and other countries. It was called the Holy Land because Jerusalem was a holy city for both Christians and Muslims

HUE AND CRY before there were policemen, if someone saw a crime, they shouted out or 'cried' and everyone who heard the cry was supposed to chase the criminal and try to catch them. The chase was known as the 'hue'

HUMOURS since the time of the ancient Greeks people believed that the body contained four important liquids called humours. People were healthy if the four humours stayed balanced but became sick if they had too much of one humour

PERSISTENT stubbornly continuing to do something

PEWTER metal made of lead mixed with tin. It was used for making plates and other crockery

PILGRIMAGE a visit (often a long and dangerous journey) to a holy site such as the tomb of St Thomas in Canterbury Cathedral or to Jerusalem

POLL TAX a tax when everyone pays the same amount

PRESSED MEN men who were kidnapped by press-gangs (groups of sailors)and forced to join the navy because there were not enough sailors

REAPER someone who cut the corn at harvest time

SCRIVENER someone who was paid to copy out documents or books by hand

ST THOMAS St Thomas Becket, Archbishop of Canterbury who was murdered by four knights in 1170 because he tried to stop King Henry II controlling the Church's laws

STATUTE OF LABOURERS a law made in 1351 which said that villeins were not allowed to become freemen and that freemen could not be paid higher wages

THE CONSTABLE AND THE WATCH the constable was a village or town official who worked part-time to keep law and order. The watchmen were his helpers

THRESHING MACHINE machine for separating the grain (which could be made into bread) from the stalks of corn

TRENCHER a platter for serving food

VILLEINS villagers who were not free. They had to work on their lord's land and could not leave the village without the lord's permissions

WAR WITH FRANCE Edward III went to war with France in 1337 because he believed he should be King of France. The war lasted until the reign of Henry VIII in the 1530s and is known as the Hundred Years War

YOKE a wooden pole carried across the shoulders so that two loads, e.g. milk pails could be carried more easily

◆ Index

THIS IS HISTORY!

◆ Titles in the series:

Pupils' Books (PB) and Teachers' Resource Books (TRB) are available for all titles.

Write Your Own Roman Story	**PB** 0 7195 7717 9	**TRB** 0 7195 7718 7
The Norman Conquest	**PB** 0 7195 8555 4	**TRB** 0 7195 8556 2
King John	**PB** 0 7195 8539 2	**TRB** 0 7195 8540 6
Lost in Time	**PB** 0 7195 8557 0	**TRB** 0 7195 8558 9
'King' Cromwell	**PB** 0 7195 8559 7	**TRB** 0 7195 8560 0
Colonialism	**PB** 0 7195 8561 9	**TRB** 0 7195 8562 7
Dying for the Vote	**PB** 0 7195 8563 5	**TRB** 0 7195 8564 3
The Trenches	**PB** 0 7195 8565 1	**TRB** 0 7195 8566 X
The Holocaust	**PB** 0 7195 7709 8	**TRB** 0 7195 7710 1
Global War	**PB** 0 7195 7711 X	**TRB** 0 7195 7712 8

◆ Acknowledgements

Photographs reproduced by kind permission of:
Cover: *main picture* George Seper/Arcaid, *detail* By permission of the British Library (Add.42130, fol.208); **p.22** *tr* By permission of the British Library (Add. 42130, fol. 170), *mr* By permission of the British Library (fol. 207v), *br* By permission of the British Library (fol.170), *tl* By permission of the British Library (fol. 176), *bl* By permission of the British Library (fol.330); **p.23** *t* By permission of the British Library (fol.202v), *m* By permission of the British Library (fol.161), *bl* By permission of the British Library (fol.158), *br* By permission of the British Library (fol.196v); **p.34** Pepys Library, Magdalene College, Cambridge; **p.35** *l* + *r* Mary Evans Picture Library, *b* Courtesy of the Museum of London; **p. 36** Courtesy of the Museum of London; **p.37** *l* By permission of the British Library (E1150/5), *r* An Eyewitness Representation of the Execution of King Charles I (1600– 49) of England, 1649 (oil on canvas) by Weesop (fl.1641–49) Private Collection/Bridgeman Art Library; **p.38** *t* Mary Evans Picture Library/Explorer, *b* Hulton Archives; **p.39** *t* Science Museum/ Science and Society Picture Library, *b* By permission of the British Library (E453/18); **p.40** *t* Hulton Archives, *b* Courtesy of the Museum of London; **p.41** *t* Oakwell Hall, Kirklees Metropolitan Council, *b* Courtesy of the Museum of London; **p.42** Mary Evans Picture Library; **p.52** *t* Oxfordshire County Council Photographic Archive, *b* © Michael Prior; **p.54** National Railway Museum/Science and Society Picture Library; **p.55** *l* + *r* Hulton Archives; **p.56** Mary Evans Picture Library; **p.57** Hulton Archives; **p.58** Mary Evans Picture Library; **p.60** The Royal Archives © HM Queen Elizabeth II; **p.61** Mary Evans Picture Library; **p.62** Mary Evans Picture Library; **p.82** City of Hereford Archaeology Unit/Mappa Mundi Trust; **p.91** John Townson/ Creation; **p.95** *l* Private Collection, *r* Supplication of the heretics, by Jean Fouquet (*c*.1425–80) Chronicle of France or of St. Denis (14th century) Bibliotheque Nationale, Paris, France/ Bridgeman Art Library; **p.100** *l* + *r* Mary Evans Picture Library; **p.101** *t* Hulton Archives, *b* National Railway Museum/Science and Society Picture Library; **p.102** *t* The Battle of Trafalgar, 21 October 1805, engraved by Thomas Sutherland for J. Jenkin's 'Naval Achievements', 1816 (engraving) by Thomas Whitcombe (*c*. 1752–1824) (after) Private Collection/The Stapleton Collection/Bridgeman Art Library, *m* The Battle of Waterloo, 18 June 1815, 1842 by G. Newton (19th century) Cheltenham Art Gallery & Museums, Gloucestershire, UK/Bridgeman Art Library, *b* Imperial Federation showing the map of the world, British Empire, by Captain JC Colombo, *c*.1886 (facsimile), Royal Geographical Society, London, UK/Bridgeman Art Library; **p.103** Provided courtesy of the Lawes Agricultural Trust Company Limited and IACR-Rothamsted; **p.104** Mary Evans Picture Library; **p.105** Public Record Office (HO42/199).

(*t* = top, *m* = middle, *b* = bottom, *l* = left, *r* = right)

Samuel Pepys and Flora Thompson text based on:
Samuel Pepys' Diary, edited by Robert Latham and William Mathews, reprinted by permission of HarperCollins Publishers Ltd
Lark Rise to Candleford, by Flora Thompson (1945), reprinted by permission of Oxford University Press.

Every effort has been made to trace all copyright holders, but if any have been inadvertently overlooked the publishers will be pleased to make the necessary arrangements at the first opportunity.